The World's Greatest Story

Church History
The First 1,000 Years

By Ken Chant

The World's Greatest Story

Church History
The First 1,000 Years

By Dr. Ken Chant

Copyright © 2012 Ken Chant

ISBN 978-1-61529-046-8

Vision Publishing
1672 Main St. E 109
Ramona, CA 92065
1-800-9-VISION
www.booksbyvision.com

All rights reserved worldwide

No part of the book may be reproduced in any manner whatsoever without written permission of the author except in brief quotations embodied in critical articles of reviews.

A NOTE ON GENDER

It is unfortunate that the English language does not contain an adequate generic pronoun (especially in the singular number) that includes without bias both male and female. So *"he, him, his, man, mankind,"* with their plurals, must do the work for both sexes. Accordingly, wherever it is appropriate to do so in the following pages, please include the feminine gender in the masculine, and vice versa.

FOOTNOTES

A work once fully referenced will thereafter be noted either by "ibid" or "op. cit."

Table of Contents

PREFACE 7

INTRODUCTION 11

PART ONE: THE PIONEER CHURCH (A.D. 100-500) 13

Chapter One: THE FOUR PERIODS
OF CHURCH HISTORY 14

Chapter Two: CAESAR CAPITULATES 31

Addendum: ON IMMUNITY FROM PERIL 53

Chapter Three: SUFFERING SAINTS 59

Chapter Four: THE TWO GREAT PERIODS
OF PERSECUTION 77

Chapter Five: CATHOLIC CHURCHES 93

Chapter Six: SINGING SAINTS 109

Chapter Seven: CHURCH CONTROVERSIES 125

**PART TWO: THE EXPANDING CHURCH
(A.D. 500-1000) 137**

Chapter Eight: MULTITUDES CONVERTED 139

Chapter Nine: PAPAL ASCENDANCY 155

Chapter Ten: PAPAL DESCENDENCY 169

Addendum: CHARISMATA ACROSS THE AGES ... 191

**PART THREE: THE UNIVERSAL CHURCH
(A.D. 1000-2000) 197**

HISTORY IS BUNK? 198

Chapter Eleven: MEDIAEVAL CHURCH 199

Chapter Twelve: MODERN CHURCH 205

BIBLIOGRAPHY 219

ABBREVIATIONS

Abbreviations commonly used for the books of the Bible are

Genesis	Ge	Habakkuk	Hb
Exodus	Ex	Zephaniah	Zp
Leviticus	Le	Haggai	Hg
Numbers	Nu	Zechariah	Zc
Deuteronomy	De	Malachi	Mal
Joshua	Js		
Judges	Jg		
Ruth	Ru	Matthew	Mt
1 Samuel	1 Sa	Mark	Mk
2 Samuel	2 Sa	Luke	Lu
1 Kings	1 Kg	John	Jn
2 Kings	2 Kg	Acts	Ac
1 Chronicles	1 Ch	Romans	Ro
2 Chronicles	2 Ch	1 Corinthians	1 Co
Ezra	Ezr	2 Corinthians	2 Co
Nehemiah	Ne	Galatians	Ga
Esther	Es	Ephesians	Ep
Job	Jb	Philippians	Ph
Psalm	Ps	Colossians	Cl
Proverbs	Pr	1 Thessalonians	1 Th
Ecclesiastes	Ec	2 Thessalonians	2 Th
Song of Songs	Ca *	1 Timothy	1 Ti
Isaiah	Is	2 Timothy	2 Ti
Jeremiah	Je	Titus	Tit
Lamentations	La	Philemon	Phm
Ezekiel	Ez	Hebrews	He
Daniel	Da	James	Ja
Hosea	Ho	1 Peter	1 Pe
Joel	Jl	2 Peter	2 Pe
Amos	Am	1 John	1 Jn
Obadiah	Ob	2 John	2 Jn
Jonah	Jo	3 John	3 Jn
Micah	Mi	Jude	Ju
Nahum	Na	Revelation	Re

Ca is an abbreviation of *Canticles*, a derivative of the Latin name of the *Song of Solomon*, which is sometimes also called the *Song of Songs*.

PREFACE

THE URBANE PHYSICIAN

One of the finest Christians of any age was the 17th. century English physician, Sir Thomas Browne. In 1643 he published the final edition of his noblest work, Religio Medici [1], which has been continuously in print ever since. It has been said that apart from Shakespeare, his was the most imaginative mind ever to appear in the British Isles. In his own day and rightly still, he was admired for the beauty of his life and character, which itself was a product of his wide reading and his love of all people. The study of history should help to build such a character in all of us.

But let Sir Thomas now speak for himself. Here are the words of a truly civilised man, and if history cannot civilise us, what can? I have modernised the spelling, but otherwise the words are just as the good physician wrote them. He had a vivid and unusual style of writing, which you may find unfamiliar, and if the going is too hard then just turn over the page! But I hope you will enjoy a brief encounter with a truly fine spirit

> "Now for that other Virtue of Charity, without which Faith is a mere notion, and of no existence, I have ever endeavoured to nourish the merciful disposition and humane inclination I borrowed from my Parents, and regulate it to the written and prescribed Laws of Charity. And if I hold the true Anatomy of myself, I am delineated and naturally framed to such a piece of virtue; for I am of a

---

1   "The Religion of a Physician"

constitution so general, that it consorts and sympathises with all things.

"I have no antipathy, or rather Idiosyncrasy, in diet, humour, air, or any thing. I wonder not at the French for their dishes of Frogs, Snails, and Toadstools, nor at the Jews for Locusts and grasshoppers; but being amongst them, make them my common Viands, and I find they agree with my Stomach as well as theirs. I could digest a Salad gathered in a Churchyard, as well as in a Garden. I cannot start at the presence of a Serpent, Scorpion, Lizard, or Salamander:[2] at the sight of a Toad or Viper, I find in me no desire to take up a stone to destroy them.[3] I feel not in myself those common Antipathies that I can discover in others: those National repugnancies do not touch me, nor do I behold with prejudice the French, Italian, Spaniard, or Dutch: but where I find their actions in balance with my Countrymen's, I honour, love, and embrace them in the same degree.

"I was born in the eighth Climate,[4] but seem for to be framed and constellated unto all. I am no Plant that will not prosper out of a Garden. All places, all airs, make unto me one Country; I am in England every where, and under any Meridian. I have been shipwrecked, yet am not enemy with the Sea or Winds; I can study, play, or sleep in a Tempest.

---

2   That is, he was not superstitious, nor given to looking for ill omens, nor to seeing misfortune predicted in natural things.

3   A fault of the 17th. century (and of many others before and since) was antagonism toward anything that was different, or was reputed to be demonised. Sir Thomas was horrified by such madness, especially when it took the form of burning of witches, and the like.

4   That is, England, which Browne reckoned lay in the eighth belt of latitude.

> "In brief, I am averse from nothing: my Conscience would give me the lie if I should say I absolutely detest or hate any essence but the Devil ... " [5]

It would be nice if at the last page of this book you too could say, I hate nothing but sin and the devil; toward all people, even those who differ from me, my heart is one of gracious charity. An understanding of history can help to achieve that admirable goal, and bring us to a fulfilment of the poet's aspiration -

> We are the music-makers,
> And we are the dreamers of dreams,
> Wandering by lone sea-breakers,
> And sitting by desolate streams;
> World-losers and world-forsakers,
> On whom the pale moon gleams;
> *Yet we are the movers and shakers*
> Of the world for ever, it seems! [6]

---

5 Religio Medici, "The Second Part," opening paragraph. The paragraph breaks shown above are mine.

6 We Are the Music-Makers, first stanza; by A. W. E. O'Shaughnessy (1844-1881), British poet and natural historian. This is usually thought to be his best poem

INTRODUCTION

HISTORY WITHOUT A HISTORIAN!

I am not an expert in church history, nor does this book have any scholarly pretensions. But I may claim to be a well-read layman, with an ability to digest what scholars far more learned than I have written, and to reproduce that material in a form useful to other lay people. So I freely acknowledge my immense debt to greater authors in the pages that follow. These pages do not contain many original ideas; yet I may fairly claim that the structure of the book and the form of its writing are my own. Some of the books from which I first began to learn church history I no longer possess, and even their titles are buried in the mists of years long past. The books upon which I have more recently depended are each identified in the various footnotes, for they are all quoted in one way or another. I will be well pleased if your reading of *these* pages persuades you to turn even more eagerly to *those*, for they will carry you with growing amazement into what is truly the world's most dramatic story!

PART ONE:

THE PIONEER CHURCH (A.D. 100-500)

Chapter One:
THE FOUR PERIODS OF CHURCH HISTORY

BREAKING BARRIERS

"All history is modern history," said Wallace Stevens.[7] That is, whatever happens today is built upon yesterday; so the better we understand the past the better we shall understand the present, and the more effectively we will be able to shape the future. Ignorance of history is lamentable, and obliges people to walk the same dark paths their ancestors have trod, like prisoners going around in a treadmill. Christian people especially should know something about the background to their faith, otherwise we shall not only repeat the follies of our fathers but also make their sufferings vain. The importance of history is endorsed by God; the Holy Spirit is himself an historian. Consider how much of the Spirit-inspired scriptures are history! In particular, the Spirit is a church-historian, composing the four *Gospels*, the *Acts of the Apostles*, and the *Apocalypse* (history in advance). We ignore biblical history and church history at our peril!

There are four major periods in church history:

    the First Millennium (to the 11th century)

    the Middle Ages (to the 16th century)

    the Reformation (to the 18th century)

---

7   American journalist, lawyer, business executive, and poet (1879-1955).

the Modern Church to the present day).

The following chapters deal with the most amazing of those periods, the *first 1000 years*, with some intrusions into the second period, followed by a brief survey of the following millennium. I have chosen to concentrate on the first ten centuries, *(a)* because most people are almost totally ignorant of what happened during those years; and *(b)* because the story they tell must surely be the world's most dramatic tale. The adventures of the new church ran the gamut of human experience, rising and falling between lofty nobility and squalid ignominy. Here we see a people collapsing from grandeur into disgrace, or rising from basest cowardice to incredible bravery. Here we find chronicles of love and hate, laughter and tears, triumph and defeat, vice and virtue, greed and generosity, failure and success. The finest and the foulest of human behaviour lie in the annals of the church; but in the end love and grace prevail, and Christ gains honour from his people. The word of the apostle is fulfilled -

> *"Unto God be glory in the church and in Jesus Christ, throughout every generation, and for ever and ever! Amen!" (Ep 3:21).*

WHY STUDY CHURCH HISTORY?

Bill Vasilakis [8] offers the following reasons -

it is fascinating: the story is exciting in its own right, with endless action, incredible exploits, marvellous heroes, unspeakable villains, and all the drama and amazement that do indeed make truth stranger than fiction!

it is satisfying: for it fulfils our deep need to understand our origins, and therefore what the present means, and what destination we shall reach as we journey toward tomorrow. Indeed, can

---

8   Unpublished lecture notes, House of Tabor, Adelaide.

anyone have any true sense of where they are going if they have no sense of where they have come from?

it provides knowledge: the doctrines that are now widely believed in all branches of the church are based nearly as much upon historical developments as they are upon scripture alone. And history has had more influence than scripture in creating the various Christian denominations. We cannot possibly understand why Christendom is so divided if we have no knowledge of the events of the past.

it brings strength: how terrible, how insuperable, how strong, were the enemies the first Christians faced as they set themselves to fulfil the Great commission. Yet they overcame even the most awful barriers, until Christianity finally became the only lawful religion in the Roman Empire. Seeing how the church overcame impossible obstacles in previous centuries greatly encourages us to believe that it will overcome those of our time.

it creates sympathy: knowing the facts of the past, we can better understand the problems confronting some churches in the present, which may make us a little less critical of others, and more aware of our own shortcomings. [9]

it imposes responsibility: gazing at the heroism, seeing the tears and toil, trembling before the bloodshed and anguish of those who preceded us, and knowing the debt we owe them, should make us more careful to pass on a good inheritance to those who will follow on our steps.

it brings instruction: the successes and failures of the past provide examples for our guidance today. We can learn from our forefathers. We are the beneficiaries of their triumphs; we bear the burden of their defeats. Their story shows us how to serve God

---

9   For example, consider the method of baptism, astonishing to us, practised in Rome in the 2nd. century - see Chapter Six below.

better, and how to crush Satan utterly. But if you don't know, how can you learn?

Any reader of these pages may be well pleased if the end result proves to be a deeper sympathy for other Christians, and for the historical processes that have brought each of us to our present place. As I have already suggested, the study of history should shape us into citizens of the world, like the chivalrous Sir Thomas Browne. [10] He dared to call himself "Christian" because he was free of the prejudices and animosities that so bitterly overshadowed much of the religious world in his 17th century -

"I dare without usurpation assume the honourable Style of a Christian. Not that I merely owe this title to the Font, my Education, or the clime wherein I was born ... but having in my riper years and confirmed Judgment seen and examined all, I find myself obliged by the Principles of Grace, and the Law of mine own Reason, to embrace no other Name but this. Neither doth herein my zeal so far make me forget the general Charity I owe unto Humanity, as rather to hate than pity Turks, Infidels, and (what is worse) Jews; rather contenting my self to enjoy that happy Style, than maligning those who refuse so glorious a Title." [11]

A similar magnanimity should mark all who name the name of Christ.

BARRIERS TO GROWTH

THE EARLY CHURCH *(30 - 500 A.D.)*

At the end of the first century, the prospects of Christianity becoming the first world-wide religion, of dramatically changing human life and culture, and of transforming the lives of more

---

10   See again the Preface above.
11   Op. cit., "The First Part", Paragraph One

individuals than any other religion in history, seemed remote. The church had to overcome apparently insuperable obstacles -

THE BARRIER OF OBSCURITY

The church was born on the Day of Pentecost, in Jerusalem in Judea, a backwater of the Roman Empire, which itself occupied but a small part of the earth's surface, and represented only one corner of civilisation. Contemporary with Rome were other more ancient and still flourishing cultures. To the immediate east was the populous and powerful empire of the Parthians, the successors of the Persians, and an implacable enemy of Rome. South lay the great land of India, whose opulence and antiquity had four centuries earlier astonished even Alexander the Great. Further east stood the immense and vastly more ancient lands of China, Japan, and the other peoples of the Orient. The achievements of their civilisations were not in the least inferior to Rome's, their luxury and grandeur surpassed even that of the Caesars. Then there were the "barbarian" hordes in northern Europe, Africa, the Americas, and the vast stretches of the Asian plateaus. Our history books (including the New Testament) may be engrossed with Rome, but in its own day it was but one of several empires, and not perhaps even the greatest of them.

Had you been a visitor from outer space, wondering which of the world's religions would prevail, you would not have chosen Christianity. Indeed, nothing would have seemed more unlikely. Without hesitation, you would have chosen perhaps the doctrines of Prince Gautama, the Buddha, whose religion was now seven centuries old, with many millions of followers. Or you might have turned to the still more ancient philosophies of Confucius, or of Lao Tse, or to the thousand-year-old faith of the prophet Zarathustra, which had millions of followers scattered throughout Persia, the Middle East, Egypt, and even among the Romans. It would have seemed to you in the highest degree improbable that the little company of Christians gathering in the Judean corner of the empire would become the source of the world's greatest religion. One might as easily think of a new religion springing up today in, say, Fiji, and expanding from there to conquer the earth! Hence Latourette writes -

> "Christianity had what looked like a most unpromising beginning. The contemporary observer outside the little inner group of the disciples of Jesus would have thought it impossible that within five centuries of its inception it would outstrip its competitors for the religious allegiance of the Roman Empire and become the professed faith of the rulers and of the overwhelming majority of the population of that realm. Still less would he have dreamed that within less than two thousand years it would become world-wide, with a more expansive geographic spread and a greater influence upon mankind than any other religion." [12]

Indeed, given the usually slow movement of history across the centuries, the growth of the church in just two millennia from twelve disciples of a crucified prophet to the most numerous of the world's religions is extraordinary. And had it remained true to its real nature and call throughout those years, its expansion would have been still more dazzling.

THE BARRIER OF RELIGION

As I have just suggested, the church had to compete with several other powerful religions, some of them new and flourishing, and others ancient and populous. There were -

THE ANCIENT PAGAN RELIGIONS

It is difficult for us to imagine the depth to which religion penetrated Greek and Roman society. The old myths and legends

---

12 A History of Christianity; Kenneth S. Latourette; Harper & Row; 1975; Vol I, pg 33

had prevailed over the lives, culture, and structure of the people for nearly a thousand years. Generations had revered Zeus of the Greeks or Jove of the Romans as the Great Father of mankind.

Long before the church was born, Greek and Roman mythology had been fused together to create an homogeneous group of deities who were honoured from one end of the empire to the other. In Egypt, the cult of Isis had persisted unbroken for twenty centuries - longer than Christianity has so far endured - and was to continue for several centuries into the Christian era.

The worship of the pagan gods was deeply established in the Graeco-Roman world, and interwoven with every aspect of society. For every human activity there was a presiding god or goddess. Religion so permeated domestic life that every corner of every house was influenced by it. For example, three deities controlled the front door, so that a placatory prayer had to be offered when the door was opened, and when the threshold was crossed, and when the door was closed. Several deities controlled the various parts of each meal, and libations, prayers, and offerings had to be made to them as the meal progressed. There were individual deities for marital intercourse, for conception, for childbirth, for lactation - and on, and on, for every event of every day, and for every part of life.

The same was true in the worlds of commerce, law, education, and government. No Roman general would dare go to war without first securing a favourable oracle from the gods. Regular great public ceremonies were held, with immense pomp and splendour, to secure heaven's favour upon the actions of the government. From the highest levels to the lowest the ancient religion was interwoven with all the affairs of the empire and of its people. The task of replacing such a centuries-old religious practice with a wholly new faith would have seemed absurdly daunting to an outside observer.

Furthermore, there was a vast difference between the religious attitudes of the Christians and the larger population. To most Greeks and Romans religion was a matter of controlling, or at least influencing, the behaviour of the gods by various rituals and sacrifices. Religion was not seen as the pathway to universal truth, let alone as a guide to morality and ethics. Those tasks were reserved for philosophy. So Christian claims that the gospel provided a total way of truth and life seemed absurdly exaggerated. A religion based upon divine revelation warred against the prevailing culture of debate and philosophical speculation. It mocked the pretensions of the glory of Greek civilisation, the academy.

JUDAISM

The worship of Yahweh, the God of Israel, was among the oldest continuous religions in the world. For nearly twenty centuries the descendants of Abraham had served the God of their fathers. By the time of the apostles, Judaism had broken out of the boundaries of Palestine and had become widely spread and honoured. The Jews alone were legally permitted to claim that their God was the sole God, and to ignore the state religion. The Jews had gained this exemption as a result of the previous four centuries, when they had shown themselves willing enough to submit to the secular rule of foreign princes, [13] but never to accept the desecration of their religion.

Josephus describes their courage -

> "They contemn the miseries of life, and are above pain, by the generosity of their mind. And as for death, if it will be for their glory, they esteem it better than living always; and indeed our war with the Romans gave abundant evidences what great souls they had in their trials, wherein, although they were tortured and distorted, burnt and torn to pieces, and went through all kinds of instruments of

---

13 Who followed each other in regular succession: Babylon, Persia, Greece, Syria, Egypt, Rome.

torment, that they might be forced either to blaspheme their legislator or to eat what was forbidden them, yet they could not be made to do either of them, no, nor once to flatter their tormentors, nor to shed a tear; but they smiled in their very pains, and laughed those to scorn who inflicted the torments upon them, and resigned up their souls with great alacrity, as expecting to receive them again." [14]

Other religions also were tolerated by the Romans, but they were required to respect the Graeco-Roman pantheon, and to be willing to participate in such formal public religious ceremonies as were deemed necessary for the welfare of the state. The Jews had gained a hard-earned exemption from that requirement and were anxious not to disturb their privileged position. Further, the stern Romans tended to admire the austere Yahweh of the Jews. They were seldom inclined to commit themselves fully to Yahwism, with its (in their view) demeaning circumcision, its dietary restraints, its many legal rules, and its exclusivism. But they were attracted by its monotheism, its dignity, its superior ethic, and its remarkable history.

Had you been asked which would triumph, the established Jewish faith, or the new and heretical Christian sect that had sprung up within it, the answer would have seemed obvious: the Jews. The Christians, like many other splinter groups, would certainly perish and be soon forgotten.

---

14 Josephus: Complete Works, "Wars of the Jews" II.8.10 ; tr. by William Whiston; 1977 reprint of the original 1867 work; Kregel Publications, Grand Rapids; pg. 477, 478. See also the astonishing and stirring story of the Jewish woman and her seven sons who were martyred by command of the tyrant Antiochus IV Epiphanes, circa 170 B.C. (2 Mc 7). They and others who perished at that time were probably the first true religious martyrs in history. Their bravery has been equalled, but never exceeded.

THE MYSTERY CULTS

Shortly before the coming of Christ a number of new religions - known generally as "mystery" cults - had sprung up. Some of the ancient faiths of the east had also begun to capture adherents in the west during the first century before the Christian era, among them the 1000-year old Persian cult of Mithras, and the 2000-year old cult of the Egyptian Isis. By the time of the apostles they had become quite popular and numbered their followers in the millions. Some of them had doctrines and practices that were strikingly similar to those of the church. In contrast with the ancient religions of the Graeco-Roman world, which were practised by the community rather than by the individual, the new cults were highly personalised. Against the impersonal civic character of the state religion, the mystery cults offered an intensely personal salvation, based upon an encounter with a divine power. This direct appeal to the individual, with a promise of a changed life, an offer of immortality, a hope of a glorious destiny, made the new cults immensely alluring to many people, and parallelled the claims of the church. In other ways too, the mystery cults contended with Christianity, especially in such rituals and dogmas as these:

- ➤ *baptism*: sometimes by immersion, sometimes by sprinkling, using water, blood, or wine;
- ➤ *love feasts* and other sacred meals that had many of the characteristics of the early Christian celebration of the eucharist;
- ➤ the *use of blood* to remove sin, sometimes by full immersion in the blood of a slaughtered bullock, and the like;
- ➤ belief in *a hero-god* who died and rose again (an idea that is expressed in some form in many of the Greek and Roman myths);

- belief that initiates could share in the ***resurrection and immortality*** of their god, and that the obedient would gain a heavenly reward;
- an ***expectation of miracles*** among those who became fully initiated into the cult and were obedient to all its mandates.
- an ***equality of status*** among full initiates that removed the harsh social barriers of the larger world.

All this was associated with a complex theology, and a strong worship practice that together provided a high level of intellectual and spiritual satisfaction to the devout.

One such cult, that of ***Mithras***, embraced nearly all the above factors, and Tertullian says that it was still flourishing at the beginning of the third century.

Was the church then just the most recent of the *"mystery"* cults, copying the ideas and methods of its predecessors? No, for the church stood absolutely apart from those cults in one thing, or should I say one person - ***Jesus***. Contrary to the mythical deities and legendary events upon which the cults were based, Jesus was a real man; his life, death, and resurrection were recorded facts; they were not lost in the mists of antiquity, but had verifiably occurred within the lifetime of the first hearers of the gospel. Beyond that, his character was unsurpassed, full of grace and dignity, unlike the bizarre and often scandalous behaviour of the cultic heroes. But above all, there was his teaching, which carried in every word the ring of truth, and showed itself instantly powerful in all who believed in him.

In another way also, the church stood apart from the mystery cults: its open invitation to all who wanted eternal life simply to embrace the gospel. The "mystery" cults were so called just because their practices were mysterious; their doctrines were revealed only to a small and privileged group of full initiates. So despite their burgeoning popularity, and the seeming inevitability of their triumph, the mystery cults were steadily overtaken and surpassed by the gospel, and eventually vanished altogether as the church gained supremacy throughout the empire.

THE CULTURAL BARRIER

The church had to face severe cultural opposition, especially because, unlike its many competitors, it did not seek to conform to the surrounding culture. In contrast with all previous world-conquerors the Romans were a tolerant people. So long as people respected Roman authority, no pressure was put on them to adopt Roman culture or religion. The effect of Roman rule was to encourage a cheerful syncretism, where a place was found for every cult, and the various deities of the conquered peoples were identified with each other - just as the Greek *Zeus* was reckoned the same as the Roman *Jove*. Attempts were made to find a common thread in all religions that would enable them to function happily under the broad umbrella of the Roman civil religion. The numerous cults freely borrowed ideas and practices from their competitors as they jostled for members.

Furthermore almost all that was joyful and beautiful in the common life of the people, the great public festivals and sporting events, theatre performances, civic ceremonies, the frequent holy days, were intertwined with prayers, libations, and sacred ceremonies of every kind.

Against such a background, the church seemed unreasonably disagreeable. Intransigent in its doctrines, refusing to compromise to the slightest degree the absolute lordship of Christ, the church made itself further disliked by its stern opposition to the most popular aspects of the surrounding culture. Such attitudes, to a contemporary watcher, would not have seemed likely to endear the church to the mass of citizens. On the contrary, it would have seemed like the Christians had deliberately chosen a policy guaranteed to lock them into insignificance and irrelevancy.

THE SOCIAL BARRIER

The origins of the church could hardly have been more obscure -

"At first sight, Jesus ... seems most unpromising for the role which has been his. He was of humble birth and was reared in an obscure village. His public career was brief. It appears at most to have been only three years, and it may have been much less. He wrote no book, nor does he seem to have given much thought toward putting his teaching into organised form. So far as our records show, he appears to have given little attention to creating a continuing organisation. He had an exalted conception of his mission and believed that in him God was beginning a new and supremely important stage in man's course, but it is at least doubtful whether he thought of himself as founding a new religion. [15] His intimate friends were drawn largely from what we today would call the lower middle class. At a crucial moment one of them betrayed him; another, their chief spokesman, denied him; and others were bewildered and disheartened. The leaders of his own people accused him of blasphemy, and on the charge that he intended to lead a revolt turned him over to the Roman procurator who, somewhat contemptuously, had him crucified between two malefactors." [16]

Hardly an auspicious beginning for a world religion! In the reckoning of those times he should at least have been born in Rome, or Athens, or one of the other great centres of civilisation. But Jerusalem? A Jew? A member of the most fractious of the conquered peoples, where some kind of sedition was always

---

15 Note the lack of certainty about the Father's purpose that Jesus showed in his prayer in the Garden of Gethsemane (Mt 26:39); also his lack of knowledge about the time of his return (Mk 13:32).

16 Latourette, from his Introduction to the article, Christianity, in "The Encyclopaedia Americana", 1959 edition.

fermenting? How could a carpenter's son, unschooled in philosophy, untrained in law or literature, unskilled in war, hope to create a movement that would shake the empire and change the face of the world? A gambling man of that time would have been unwilling to make even a small wager on the success of the church!

THE BARRIER OF MISUNDERSTANDING

At the cross the highest religion and the best government the world had known to that time conspired in hatred to kill Christ. Jew and Roman joined hands to murder the one who had come from God to save them both. It was a microcosm of the history of the church. Sadly, across the centuries not just the worst of men have persecuted the church, but also the best. Some of the finest of earth's rulers have risen up in hatred against Christianity and striven to destroy it. A notable example can be seen in the emperor Marcus Aurelius. A Stoic philosopher, he reigned from 161-181, and under his rule Justin Martyr, Polycarp, Pothinus, and many others were put to death. They were reckoned to have committed treason against the state. Marcus himself endeavoured to be impartial in his sanction of persecution; but some of the provincial governors were motivated by avarice and fear, and were more violent than the emperor would have readily allowed.

Nonetheless, by his authority the church was persecuted, which was a double misfortune; for it is universally acknowledged that no throne has ever been occupied by a nobler man. Marcus Aurelius is known today mostly for a remarkable diary, called "Meditations", that was found after his death. He did not intend anyone other than himself to read its pages, which are filled with observations on life and admonitions to himself to live more nobly. From the day of its discovery the "Meditations" has never been out of circulation. Multitudes of people in many nations and languages have turned to it for challenge and inspiration. You may glean something of the character of its author from the following quotes -

> "A man should <u>be</u> upright, not be <u>kept</u> upright ... Never esteem anything as of advantage to you that will make you break your word or lose your self-respect ... How much time he gains who does not look to see what his neighbour says or does or thinks, but only at what he does himself, to make it just and holy ... Love the little trade which you have learned, and be content with it ... There is a proper dignity and proportion to be observed in the performance of every act of life ... A good man makes no noise over a good deed, but passes on to another as a vine to bear grapes again in season ... It is man's peculiar duty to love even those who wrong him."

How tragic that a man who could write such words completely misunderstood the church, and thought it necessary to obliterate the Christian faith! But that very nobility and temperate austerity made him look with antagonism upon the zealous and disruptive church. He was himself waging war on the frontiers of the empire, defending it against barbarian onslaughts, and Christians seemed to him to be turbulent fanatics who were a menace to the security of the state. So under his authority there were two main bursts of persecution, which brought violent death to two great Christian leaders: in the first, Polycarp [17] perished in 166; and in the second, in 177, Bishop Pothinus of Lyons, and an unknown number of others, men, women, and young people, also perished miserably.

---

17 See the fine description in Eusebius Bk. IV ch. 15. After he had been arrested and the governor commanded him to revile Christ, he said: "I have served Christ for 86 years, and he never did me any wrong. How can I now blaspheme the King who saved me?" He resisted cheerfully and bravely all threats and violence, until he was finally run through with a sword and burnt at the stake. But his great age, his courage, the absurdity of the charges laid against him, the loud protest of the large number of Christians, all ensured that he was the last martyr in that persecution

It has been sadly true throughout the long history of the church that just as many fine people have scorned its message as have the wicked. The good news of God's free grace offered to the worst of us through the crucified One, the miracle of his resurrection and ascension, the promise of his return, the assurance of resurrection from the dead - all have often seemed impossible, if not scandalous, even to people of goodwill. So the preaching of the church has been misunderstood, her motives misrepresented, her methods misconstrued, and her mission misinterpreted. Thus the church, like her Lord, has been crucified. But if the church shares in the dying of Christ, she also shares in his resurrection, and has proved as indestructible as he is! In the end, that is our only true victory - not that we transform the face of society, but that the great leveller of all, godly and ungodly alike, has no lasting victory over the church of Jesus Christ -

> The glories of our blood and state
> Are shadows, not substantial things;
> There is no armour against fate;
> Death lays his icy hand on kings:
>
> Sceptre and Crown
> Must tumble down,
> And in the dust be equal made
> With the poor crooked scythe and spade.
>
> The garlands wither on your brow,
> Then boast no more your mighty deeds;
> Upon death's purple altar now
> See, where the victor-victim bleeds:
>
> Your heads must come
> To the cold tomb;
> Only the actions of the just
> Smell sweet, and blossom in their dust! [18]

---

18 James Shirley (1596-1666), English cleric, dramatist, and poet; first and last stanzas.

Chapter Two:
CAESAR CAPITULATES

THE MISSIONARY OUTREACH OF THE EARLY CHURCH

The French emperor Napoleon III, having completed a history on the life of *Julius Caesar*, and intending to give a copy of the book to his young son, first asked another historian, the German writer Mommsen, for an opinion.

> "How old is the boy?" asked Mommsen.
>
> "Fourteen."
>
> "Good, give it to him now," said the German. "One more year and he'll be too old for it!"
>
> Likewise Euripides, the Greek dramatist (480-406 B.C.), insisted, "Whoso neglects learning in his youth loses the past and is dead for the future."

No doubt it is wise to learn history when one is young, and hopefully still able to learn from it. What follies I have seen over 40 years of ministry, which could have been avoided if only every young pastor had been obliged to immerse himself in church history before launching out into ministry!

Nonetheless, it is surely better to learn history when one is older than not at all. So whether young or old, the wisdom of the Greek historian Thucydides (c. 460-c. 400 B.C.) remains true: "An exact knowledge of the past is an aid to the interpretation of the future." [19] But how to obtain that knowledge?

---

19 In the Introduction to his History of the Peloponnesian War, Bk. I, Sec 1.

One way to study the history of the church is to isolate its characteristics, and then trace each one separately across the centuries. I plan to use that approach, and to look in sequence at how various things developed in the church during its first 500 years. We will be exploring one by one each of the following aspects:

- Missionary Outreach
- Persecutions
- Government
- The Local Church
- The Charismata
- Doctrines

Let me begin then with the story of the missionary work and expansion of the church until the end of the fifth century.

THE FIRST CENTURY (A.D 35-100)

Our best, and almost our only, source of information about the church during those first few decades is the New Testament. What the *Acts of the Apostles* begins to describe continued with little change to the end of the century. There was growth, there was persecution, there were triumphs and defeats. Some doctrinal quarrels were solved, but new ones developed. Debate began about how the churches should be organised. Problems arose in connection with baptism, and the eucharist, and with itinerant ministries, as this quaint passage from the *"Didache"* shows - [20]

---

[20] "Didache" means "The Teaching", and the full name of the work is "The Teaching of the Lord to the Gentiles by the Twelve Apostles." It was composed around the year 100 as a manual of practical instruction, and deals with a variety of themes, such as Christian virtue, water baptism, the eucharist, itinerant prophets, and the like. It was lost for centuries, but then discovered in 1873 in the library of a Constantinople monastery.

"Concerning Baptism, this is how you should proceed. If the people have been well-instructed, then baptise them in running water, in the name of the Father, and of the Son, and of the Holy Spirit. If you cannot find running water, then use still water, which should be cold if possible, but if not, then warm...

"Concerning the Eucharist, this is how you should give thanks. Begin with the chalice ... (and then) ... take the broken bread ... You must not allow anyone to share in the Eucharist who has not been baptised in the name of the Lord, for the Lord himself said, `You must not give to the dogs things that are holy'...

"Concerning travelling apostles and prophets, you should follow the instructions of the Gospel. So let every apostle be received as you would welcome the Lord himself. But he ought not to remain with you for more than a day, or two at the most; if he remains for three days, then he is a false prophet. And when an apostle leaves you, he should take no more than he needs to get him to his next lodging. If he asks for more money, he is a false prophet.

"When a prophet speaks in the spirit, do not interrupt him with questions, or try to verify what he is saying, for *every sin can be forgiven except this one'*. Yet not everyone who speaks in the spirit is a prophet, unless he also walks in the ways of the Lord. By each prophet's behaviour you will be able to separate the true from the false. For example, if a

> prophet speaking in the spirit demands food, he will not eat it; if he does, he is a fraud." [21]

Somewhere near the end of the century, after the apostle John had died, many people left the church. They were disappointed because Christ had not returned, as they thought he had promised to do. [22] But the church was not seriously weakened; its numbers were soon restored; and it entered the second century with a good foundation laid for strong growth.

THE SECOND CENTURY

Following the death of the last apostle, the rate of change in the church accelerated. Strong leaders arose who endeavoured to impose upon the growing number of congregations some kind of orderly cohesion. The appearances of false doctrine from time to time obliged the churches to draw together for self protection. Leadership by apostles and prophets was replaced more and more by the administrative rule of bishops and other ecclesiastics. The group of orthodox churches (that is, those who remained within the main-stream) assumed more of the shape and character of what we today would call a *denomination*. Alongside that far more numerous orthodox body a variety of small sects sprang up, each protesting that the main churches had already begun to depart from the faith, and each claiming to preach a purer doctrine.

During the second century, worship practices became more standardised, liturgies were developed, doctrine was formalised, and rules of life were imposed. The first attempts were made to establish the limits of scripture; that is, to determine which apostolic writings should be joined with the Hebrew scriptures to form a new Christian Bible. The second century also produced the

---

[21] Adapted from several sources, including Early Christian Writings, tr. Maxwell Staniforth; Penguin Books, London, 1968; pg. 232 ff.; and the Ante-Nicene Fathers, Vol. VII; Eerdmans Pub. Co., 1978 reprint.

[22] Compare Matthew 16:27-28; 24:34,44; John 21:22-23; etc.

first outbreaks of serious persecution of the church by the Roman authorities. The violence, however, remained spasmodic and mostly restricted to particular localities. So through it all, the number of Christians within the empire and beyond it continued to increase steadily. By the end of its first full century of witness (circa 150) the church, while still a minority of the population (probably still less than ten per cent), had become influential enough to command attention at all levels of society.

Nevertheless, this remains a largely silent century. Some writings of the Fathers are still extant, and a few references to Christianity can be found among secular documents of the time. But on the whole we have little detailed knowledge of the history of the church during this period.

Early in the second century the church had already become disentangled from its Jewish roots. The reasons for this are not altogether clear, apart from the antagonism of the Jewish leaders; still, for better or worse, the church was no longer perceived as a Jewish sect, but as a completely new religion. That had the disadvantage of removing from Christians the legal advantages under which Judaism operated; but it also had the advantage of removing from the church the restraints of being identified with a particular race and culture. Christians were able to adopt the best of both worlds. They embraced elements of Judaism, such as the Hebrew scriptures; they copied the pattern of worship used in the Jewish synagogues; they gave preaching a major place in their services; and the like. But they were also now free to embrace elements of the surrounding Hellenistic culture, especially in governmental structures, in the terminology they used to describe their officers, and in the manner of formulating and expressing their growing body of doctrine.

During this century the church remained predominantly urban in character, spreading out across the empire from city to city, along the common trade routes, and only gradually beginning the task of evangelising the surrounding countryside. This steady process was facilitated by the *Pax Romana* (which endured virtually undisturbed for some 200 years). [23] Roman hegemony over the lands surrounding the Mediterranean had created an unparalleled window of opportunity, one that had never existed before, and, with the collapse of the empire, would not exist again for many centuries. But before that window closed, the church had become sufficiently established to withstand the fiercest battering.

Truly, as Paul had said, Christ came just when "the time was ripe" (Ga 4:4). Any sooner would have been too soon; any later would have been too late; and the church would not have been successfully planted. [24] But when Octavian Caesar made himself the first emperor of the Romans, the scene was finally set for the proclamation of the gospel. When the apostles sallied forth they found a world ready, as it had never been before, and seldom since, to hear their message. The time was right in a number of ways -

The Time was Right for the Church.

---

[23] "There have been perhaps a score of battles, of which it may truly be said that they mark a turning point in history. The sea-battle which was fought off the west coast of Greece in the afternoon of 2 September, 31 B.C., was certainly one. In the battle of Actium Antony was finally defeated; within the year he and Cleopatra were dead, and Octavian, the heir of Julius Caesar, was master of the world. A century of civil strife was brought to an end, the arch of Janus was shut as a sign of peace abroad, and two centuries of Pax Romana had begun." (Publius Vergilius Maro, The Georgics - Introduction; tr. K. R. Mackenzie; The Folio Society, London, 1969; pg. 5.)

A similar scenario was repeated in the 19th century, when under the "Pax Britannica" there was an extraordinary growth in world-wide missionary endeavour.

[24] If you doubt the influence of the social environment over the preaching of the gospel, consider the various lands in our own time in which the church finds it impossible to secure any strong growth - such as Japan, several Islamic countries, India, etc. Of course, conditions in those countries may change, as it has in others; but for the moment they are not amenable to successful penetration by the gospel.

SPIRITUALLY

After a thousand years of reverence, the old paganism was everywhere dying. The ancient myths, mocked by playwrights, poets, and philosophers, had lost their power. An alternative had been provided by the Jews, who had built synagogues in every city (Ac 15:21). Their austere monotheism was appealing; but most people found it too exclusive, too much tainted by ethnic trappings, too harsh in its physical and cultural demands. So there remained a world-wide hunger for a better understanding of God and a better way to find him. That hunger was linked with an expectation that the time was ripe for a great Deliverer to arise. Thus the Roman historian Suetonius, in his *Life of Vespasian*, wrote -

> "An ancient superstition was current in the East, that out of Judea would come the rulers of the world."

People everywhere were wondering if perhaps that new King would come soon? The apostles declared that in fact he had *already* come, and now salvation for everyone who believed was offered in his name.

CULTURALLY

The conquests of Alexander the Great 400 years earlier had spread the Greek language, and its art, civilisation, and literature, throughout the world. The Romans acknowledged the superiority of Greek culture, and encouraged its dissemination throughout their empire. By the time of the apostles Greek was everywhere either spoken or understood. [25] So the apostles had a vehicle of communication that could be understood from one end of the

---

[25] Latin was the language of law and government; native tongues were spoken at home and among ethnic friends; but Greek was the language of international commerce, travel, philosophy, and communication. Thus, when Christ was crucified, the charge against him was written in Latin, Aramaic, and Greek.

empire to the other, transcending the often insuperable barriers of tongue and culture. This cultural and linguistic homogeneity - which had never before existed on such a wide scale - endured for only a brief period - but it was long enough for the gospel to be carried to the ends of the civilised world.

POLITICALLY

The genius of the *Greeks* lay in their art and literature; the *Jews* were uniquely gifted in religious insight; but the skill of the *Romans* was expressed in government and law. By the time of the apostles the principles of Roman jurisprudence had become firmly established throughout the empire, and provided an example that made the forensic ideas of the gospel (with its message of justification by faith) everywhere comprehensible. Perhaps only a hundred years before Paul was born, his letters to the *Romans* and to the *Galatians* would have been at best dimly understood and at worst meaningless. But when those letters were written in the second half of the first century, and then during the next hundred years carried to the furthest reaches of the empire, they made a powerful impact. To a people familiar with Roman law and government, Paul's arguments were irresistible. By the time that government collapsed and its laws were overthrown, the work was done. The legal basis upon which the gospel stands was too deeply rooted in Christian theology, and in the culture of the church, to be destroyed.

PRACTICALLY

A century before Paul began his mission Julius Caesar had purged the Mediterranean of pirates, so that apart from the ordinary perils of the deep, sea travel had been rendered safe. The Roman fleet prowled the pathways of the ocean, allowing countless other vessels to sail safely to and fro, carrying freight and passengers - including the messengers of Christ.

Likewise, the Roman army had threaded the empire with splendid paved roads, which were guarded by a chain of military forts. For the first time in history this made surface travel safe for ordinary people.[26] Again, this umbrella of naval and military protection lasted only while the empire remained strong. But it was long enough to enable the early missionaries to journey constantly and freely, by land and sea, carrying the good news wherever they went.

SOCIALLY

With the emperor Augustus there began an era of 300 years of comparative peace unparalleled in the ancient world.[27] The nature of the gospel is such that it cannot be successfully promulgated in times of shattering social disorder. Wars and riots are deleterious to the proclamation of the good news of peace and prosperity (cp. 1 Ti 2:2-3). But Roman hegemony, while it lasted, brought quietness to a war-weary world, and enabled hundreds, even thousands, of churches to be planted, and a multitude of people to be firmly discipled in the ways of Christ.

This process was also assisted by the strongly laissez-faire structure of Roman society at that time. Anyone was free to pursue any career he or she chose, and to live wherever they pleased. Later, as the empire began to crumble administratively, fiscally, and politically, various laws were passed to lock people into a particular profession, and even to prevent them from moving to another locality. But by then the church was established throughout the known world. The hour of opportunity had been

---

26 By contrast, note Sirach's brave comment, only two centuries earlier: "A person who is well-travelled learns many things, and knows what he is talking about ... In the course of my own travels ... I have often faced fearful perils, and had to depend entirely upon my own good wits to save me" (Sir 34:9-12).

27 The "Pax Romana" brought to an end centuries of constant warfare. The citizens of the empire were so grateful for its benefits, that they readily called Caesar the "Saviour" of the world (which is one reason why the term is seldom used in the New Testament).

well exploited, and the subsequent laws were helpless to hinder the continued growth of Christianity. [28]

Most of all, however, the rapid spread of the gospel was assisted by a universal spiritual hunger that then existed. This yearning for spiritual reality was caused by factors like the following -

Masses of people suffered a loss of personal identity and sense of worth when thousands of small communities were absorbed into the vast empire. Families whose horizon had scarcely extended past their own village, and whose experience of life had been confined to one culture, suddenly found themselves thrown into a maelstrom of competing ideas and practices. Men and women who had once held a place of some significance in their own small communities of a few score people, were reduced to the low state of unimportant members of a population in excess of 200 million. Indeed, Rome homogenised its citizens socially and culturally in a way that no other empire had ever done. It was hard for ordinary people to see any meaning or value in their lives when they were helpless even to modify let alone control the shape of their world. Therefore, since they could find no value for themselves in this world, perhaps it could be found in a higher dimension?

Former social and religious ties were severed when masses of people were uprooted and shifted to various parts of the empire, whether by their own choice, or by some government decree. The effect on religion was particularly drastic, since most gods and goddesses were linked to a particular locality, and their worshippers had no assurance that such deities could travel. Even if it was believed that a pagan god *could* still hear prayer at a distance, there was no certainty of an answer. Most gods were jealous of their territory, and would resent, and probably oppose, interference by a deity who belonged elsewhere! So the hunger

---

28 The occasional bursts of imperial persecution of the church did not significantly alter this situation.

grew for a God who could transcend all barriers of space and time, of culture and place.

The old religions, worn out with age, had lost vitality. Whatever power they may have once possessed to stir human imagination and to satisfy the soul's hunger was now long dissipated. Further, they had become increasingly discredited as people learned about the multitude of deities and myths revered in different parts of the empire. Questions were asked: who then *is* the supreme deity - *Zeus* of the Greeks, *Jove* of the Romans, *Yahweh* of the Jews, *Osiris* of the Egyptians? Do any of them actually exist? Is any of them the real Creator? The world was ready for a demonstrated proof that there is truly one loving, all-powerful, all-caring Father of every person.

Among the host of decent people there was a growing revulsion against the rising immorality of the times, and the collapse of the old standards of virtue. Tertullian drew attention to this, in his comment on the incidence of divorce among the Romans -

> "So true, moreover, is it that divorce `was not from the beginning' among the Romans it is not until after the six hundredth year from the building of the city that this kind of `hardheartedness' is set down as having been committed. But (now) they indulge in promiscuous adulteries, even without divorcing (their partners) ... " [29]

Formerly, people had found a sense of permanence in the stability, generation after generation, of their tribal, family, or social unit. A man looked back to his forefathers, and then forward to his children and grandchildren; and in that unbroken line, all dwelling in the same village, he gained a strong sense of worth, of place in the great scheme of things, of personal continuity. But the demands and opportunities of empire had created a society far

---

[29] "On Monogamy" ch. 10; Ante-Nicene Fathers Vol IV; pg. 66.

more mobile than had ever before existed. Now people could look only to themselves and their immediate families. Suddenly life seemed all too short. For the first time masses of people began to think seriously about the possibility of immortality. Just what *does* death mean? Can one actually survive the grave? If so, what then? Into that scene came the gospel, declaring that life and immortality were God's gift to all who believe, through the One who himself had conquered death, Jesus Christ.

From our perspective the above survey is doubly fascinating, because all the ingredients that made the world ready to hear the apostles when the apostles began their missionary forays are once again present. Look back over those items, and you will not find it difficult to see how the time is set anew for the proclamation of Christ in a world that desperately needs to re-discover spiritual reality.

There was another, and not so fortunate, similarity between those times and ours. The same conditions that created a spiritual climate favourable for the preaching of the gospel also favoured the growth of many other new cults. These were mainly born in the east, and they too had begun to spread rapidly throughout the empire. Among them were the Persian cult of Zarathustrianism and other oriental religions that for a time were serious rivals of the church. Indeed, there was a fairly extended period during which an observer might reasonably have supposed that one of those other faiths would triumph, and that the church would perish. When the apostles first began to preach, the followers of Zarathustra already numbered many millions, and his cult was especially popular among the influential military legions. Simple in concept, plain in doctrine, appealing in its morality, enticing in its promise, Zarathustrianism for a time must have seemed the most likely religion to capture the hearts of the people.

But it was not to be. Throughout the century the church continued to grow until, by the year 200, it had reached the furthest bounds of the empire and had even gone into many lands that lay outside Rome's control. Christians were still a definite minority, but a very visible one; the old paganism was still the religion of the majority, but its grip was weakening, and tens of thousands had forsaken it for one of the new faiths. But now even those new faiths were being compelled to give way before the growing dominance of the church.

THE THIRD CENTURY

GREGORY THAUMATURGOS

The third century witnessed a phenomenal expansion of the church. By its end there were probably as many as 200 bishoprics in Italy alone. Even in distant Gaul to the far west the church was now well established, and the gospel had crossed the channel and was beginning to flourish in Britain. To the east, the church was now strongly established among the Parthians, was pressing south into Arabia, expanding across Egypt and north Africa, and may even have crossed the Himalayas into India. The first known church building is dated from this century; it was discovered in Syria, and was in use around 230 A.D. [30]

Let the story of *Gregory Thaumaturgos* [31] be an example of the entire period -

He was born in Pontus, Asia Minor, around the year 210, of wealthy and socially prominent parents. His father died when he was 14, but his mother was determined that her son should not suffer by the loss. She was ambitious for him to fulfil his proper station in life, so she secured for him the best possible education, and sent him abroad to study under the greatest scholars.

---

30 The first Christians commonly used either homes (Ro 16:5) or rented halls (Ac 19:9).

31 "Thaumaturgos" comes from the Greek word for a "healer"; an appellation that Gregory received because of the numerous miraculous cures that were attributed to him.

During those travels he met the renowned Christian teacher, Origen. Gregory was so impressed by Origen's piety and learning that he remained with him for five years.[32] During that period, and against the teaching of his father who had earlier instilled into him pagan concepts, Gregory was converted to Christ.

When Gregory finally returned to his native city (c. 240), the fame of his godliness and oratory had gone before him. There were soon demands that (despite being only 30 years old) he should be made bishop, a task he was most reluctant to embrace. So he went into hiding. But the people would not be denied, and with all the usual pomp and ceremony, he was ordained bishop *in absentia*. Yielding to the inevitable, Gregory came out of hiding and accepted the sacred office.

He served as bishop for some 30 years, until his death, and was immensely successful. He won the whole region to Christ, and was renowned for the astonishing miracles that were said to have been wrought by him. Perhaps with some exaggeration, the claim was made that when he began his ministry in Pontus there were only 17 Christians; but when he died, there were only 17 pagans![33]

Gregory was one of the first leaders to recognise the needs of the people for social functions that were compatible with their faith, so he shrewdly replaced several pagan festivals with Christian equivalents. Thus he avoided the dilemma of trying to uproot immensely popular celebrations, and he also provided easy

---

32   He had little choice about the five years, for Origen insisted upon three years of instruction in grammar, logic, and philosophy, before he would allow his students even to begin any theological training! For more on Origen, see Chapter Four below.

33   The story goes that when he first arrived in Pontus he gathered the 17 Christians together for prayer, then took them out onto the streets to invite the sick to come for healing. Many miracles occurred, and the church began to grow. On his deathbed, when he enquired about the state of the church he was leaving, he was told that there were now left only as many heathen as he had first found Christians in Pontus.

occasions for Christians to mingle together in dance, song, and feasting.

Basil of Caesarea, who lived 100 years later, has left us this description of the remarkable Gregory:

> "But where shall I rank the great Gregory, and the words uttered by him? Shall we not place among the Apostles and Prophets a man who walked by the same spirit as they, who never through all his days diverged from the footprints of the saints, who maintained as long as he lived, the exact principles of evangelical citizenship? ... (By) the fellow-working of the Holy Spirit the power that he had over demons was tremendous, and so gifted was he with the grace of the word ... that, although seventeen Christians were handed over to him, he brought the whole people alike in town and country through knowledge to God ... To recount all his wonderful works in detail would be too long a task. By the superabundance of gifts, wrought in him by the Spirit in all power and in signs and marvels, he was styled a second Moses by the very enemies of the church..."[34]

During the time of Gregory, Rome began to suffer the barbarian invasions that within 300 years would destroy the western segment of the empire.[35] During those terrible times of upheaval for the peoples of Europe, the church alone remained a bastion of social stability. For example, after an invasion of his country by the Goths (circa 260), who had plundered the homes of the people,

---

[34] Nicene and Post-Nicene Fathers, "Second Series, Vol 8; Eerdmans Publishing Co.; 1978 reprint; "Treatise on the Holy Spirit," ch 29, sec 74 (pages 46,47). For a list of Gregory's reputed miracles, see Ante-Nicene Fathers, Vol 6, pg 6, footnote 3.

[35] The last western emperor was Augustulus Romulus, who reigned 475-476.

enslaved many of them, and raped many of the women, Gregory wrote a letter to all the churches under his authority. His words show great compassion, yet also a determination to maintain discipline and order. Here are some parts of that letter. The first selection deals with eating the food of the barbarians, and with the captured women - [36]

"The meats are no burden to us ... if the captives ate things which their conquerors set before them ... (for Christ) who cleanseth all meats saith: 'Not that which goeth into a man defileth the man, but that which cometh out.' And this meets the case of the captive women defiled by the barbarians, who outraged their bodies."

He goes on to say that virtuous women were to be reckoned still virtuous, no matter what their captors had compelled them to do; but the same indulgence was not to be shown to women who had been known to have loose morals before they were captured.

In the same letter, Gregory deals with those who came after the invaders, and foully looted the empty houses and goods of their neighbours -

> " ... that at the time of the irruption, in the midst of such woeful sorrows and bitter lamentations, some should have been audacious enough to consider the crisis which brought destruction to all the very period for their own private aggrandisement, that is a thing which can be averred only of men who are impious and hated of God, and of unsurpassable iniquity. Wherefore it seemed good to excommunicate such persons, lest the wrath of God should come upon the whole people, and upon those first of all who are set over them in office, and yet fail to make enquiry ... Let no one deceive himself, nor put

---

[36] Thousands of Christian wives and maidens brutally raped? Is that possible? Could it happen again? See the Addendum at the end of this chapter.

forward the pretext of having found such property. For it is not lawful, even for a man who has found anything, to aggrandise himself by it ... But others deceive themselves by fancying that they can retain the property of others which they may have found, as an equivalent for their own property which they have lost. In this way, verily, just as the Boradi and Goths brought the havoc of war on them, they make themselves Boradi and Goths to others ... "

The letter goes on, sternly denouncing other local people who in one way or another had made themselves traitors by co-operating with the invaders, even showing them the way to their neighbour's houses, and taking up arms with the Goths against their neighbours. Such persons, said Gregory, were to be utterly barred from the church. [37]

So, in the example of the great bishop Gregory, and the rapidly expanding churches he ruled so well in Asia-Minor, we see a picture of what was happening throughout the empire during the third century. There was both triumph and tragedy, abounding joy and wailing sorrow, prosperous peace and hideous invasion. But the church was now too strong to be destroyed, and through every vicissitude it continued to grow.

By the end of the third century perhaps as many as one tenth of the entire population of the empire was now Christian. However, since most churches were still in the larger cities - with only a few in rural areas - the proportion of Christians among the urban population was considerably higher, perhaps as much as a quarter or more..

---

[37] "Canonical Epistle"; Ante-Nicene Fathers, Vol 6, pg 18-19.

FOURTH & FIFTH CENTURIES

Constantine, the first Christian emperor, became master of the Roman dominions in 324, and at once put an end to all persecution. His policy was to tolerate all religions, and to persecute none. He did increasingly favour the church, but he did not proscribe other faiths, some of which continued to flourish. However, under his successors [38] increasing restraints were placed upon the practice of the old paganism, and the church was given an ever more privileged position, until (as we shall see) by the end of the 4th century it was made the state religion of the empire.

Still, during the 4th century the struggles with paganism were certainly not ended. Christians were probably still outnumbered by pagans, and the old faiths continued strong throughout the empire, especially in rural areas. Some of those former religions, after being purged of their worst follies, even enjoyed a "revival". Throughout the reign of Constantine, and after, the majestic pagan temples still stood in Rome, the high priest was still one of the great officials in the empire. The final victory of the church, to an outside observer, would still have seemed less than assured.

But as the empire continued to collapse under barbarian attacks, the church increasingly became the only stable and empire-wide institution, especially in the west. Its bishoprics, dioceses, parishes, were modelled on those of the civil administration (even to using the same names and titles), so that where the civil power was destroyed the church was able to step in with its own recognisable organisation and government. Its structures and officers sounded familiar to the people, who readily yielded secular power to the now influential bishops.

---

[38] With the exception of the brief reign of his nephew, Julian the Apostate, who ruled for less than three years. He was mortally wounded in a battle against the Parthians, and according to tradition his last words were, "Vicisti Galilaee!" ("Thou hast conquered, O Galilean!")

In the vain hope of attracting divine support against the invaders, a despairing government enacted more and more sanctions against the pagans. [39] Consequently, since few pagans were willing to die for their faith, or even suffer imprisonment or a fine, the church swelled rapidly in numbers, and waxed mighty in wealth and power. The vastly increased strength of the church at the beginning of the 5th century is graphically highlighted by a clash between bishop Ambrose of Milan and the powerful emperor Theodosius the Great (346-395) -

AMBROSE AND THEODOSIUS THE GREAT

When Ambrose was still an infant, a swarm of bees settled on his face, without harming him, and this was seen as a sign that he would become a great orator. So upon reaching adult life, after a fine education, he chose the career of a lawyer and advocate. He was working as a civil servant in this capacity when the bishopric of Milan became vacant. He was striving to act as a peacemaker between two rival factions when a child's voice spoke out of the crowd saying, `Ambrose shall be bishop!' Everyone took this as a word from heaven, and although Ambrose was not yet baptised, and against his vigorous protests, he was elected bishop.

He was a forceful and eloquent advocate for the church, and became a confidant of the emperor himself. However, one day, in a fit of anger against a rioting mob, Theodosius commanded his troops to slaughter thousands of them. It was an act of foul murder that horrified an increasingly civilised and gentler world. Ambrose excommunicated the emperor, and would not allow him to enter the cathedral until he had done public penance.

Here is how the historian Edward Gibbon (1737-94) described the scene -

---

[39] There is a lesson here for those who still want the government to legislate the gospel. You can't buy divine approval by enacting a body of law, not even laws that favour the church.

"The people of Thessalonica were treacherously invited, in the name of their sovereign, to the games of the circus ... As soon as the assembly was complete, the soldiers, who had been secretly posted round the circus, received the signal, not of the races, but of a general massacre. The promiscuous carnage continued three hours, without discrimination of strangers or natives, of age or sex, of innocence or guilt; the most moderate accounts state the number of the slain at seven thousand; and it is affirmed by some writers that more than fifteen thousand victims were (slaughtered) ...

"When Ambrose was informed of the massacre of Thessalonica, his mind was filled with horror and anguish. He retired into the country to indulge his grief and to avoid the presence of Theodosius. But as the archbishop was satisfied that a timid silence would render him the accomplice of his guilt, he represented in a private letter the enormity of the crime, which could only be effaced by tears of penitence. ...

"The emperor was deeply affected, and after he had bewailed the mischievous and irreparable consequences of his rash fury, he proceeded in his accustomed manner to perform his devotions in the great church of Milan. He was stopped in the porch by the archbishop, who, in the tone and language of an ambassador of Heaven, declared to his sovereign that private contribution was not sufficient to atone for a public fault or to appease the justice of the offended Deity. Theodosius humbly represented that, if he had contracted the guilt of homicide, David, the man after God's own heart, had been guilty not only of murder but of adultery. `You have imitated David in his crime, imitate then his repentance,' was the reply of the undaunted Ambrose. The rigorous conditions of peace and pardon were accepted; and the public penance of the emperor Theodosius has been recorded as one of the most honourable events in the annals of the church." [40]

Across the next 100 years the church continued to increase in numbers, wealth, and power, so that by the year 500, Christianity was the professed religion of the overwhelming majority of the people in all parts of the empire. Even the invading, and now (in many places) ruling barbarians, could not resist the pervasive influence of the church; they themselves were soon christianised, though perhaps not fully converted.

Nonetheless, the church could reasonably claim that Caesar had capitulated to Christ.

---

[40] Gibbon's Decline and Fall of the Roman Empire, abridged by Rosemary Wilson; Bison Books Ltd, London, 1991; pg. 190.

Addendum:
ON IMMUNITY FROM PERIL

Many Christians find a cluster of promises in scripture that seem to promise a high level of divine protection from all kinds of perils - accidents, theft, assault, rape, murder, and the like. [41] They give absolute strength to those promises and are convinced that evil could touch them only through a window of unbelief. So long as they stand firm in faith they reckon themselves inviolate from the dangers that threaten other people. No thief can break into their home; no rapist can assault their women-folk; no accident can maim them on the freeway; no fire or flood can reach their dwelling - are they not protected by the Almighty?

We may readily agree that there is a general promise of protection, peace, prosperity, given to the children of God. But the promise cannot be turned into an inflexible guarantee, because there are too many other scriptures that modify it. The Bible itself shows that God's people are not immune from the ordinary vicissitudes of life. For example:

- ➢ Baruch was told that he could not escape the general misfortune that was about to fall upon his people (Je 45:5); he was part of the community, and therefore must be as willing to share in its sorrows as in its blessings;

- ➢ hence among the thousands who were tortured, raped, murdered, and enslaved when Jerusalem was overthrown by the Babylonians, there were many good and God-fearing people, young and old, including innocent children (see *Lamentations*);

---

[41] De 33:27; Ps 18:2; 32:7; 36:7; 61:3; 91:5-12; 121:7; Pr 12:21; 18:10; and many others.

- Jesus warned against setting your heart too much on worldly treasures, because any of them can be attacked by *"moth, rust, and thieves"* (Mt 6:19), and in this world we may expect suffering (Jn 16:33);
- Jesus predicted that wars, famines, earthquakes, floods, pestilences, persecutions, would all be part of this world right up until the kingdom of God dawns; nor did he ever suggest that Christians could escape the ill effects of these ongoing *"birth-pangs"* of the coming age (Mt 24:4-13; Lu 21:10-12);
- the apostles told Christians that they must learn how to suffer bitter wrong (including sexual assault, fraud, theft, extortion), even by fellow "Christians", let alone by the world (1 Co 6:7-10), and that true saints know how to accept cheerfully public abuse, assault, and the violent seizure of all their goods (He 10:32-34).

Such scriptures and comments could be multiplied many times over. History confirms that Christians have no inviolable promise of protection from life's vicissitudes. The fate that overwhelmed the church in the time of Gregory Thaumaturgos has often beset Christian people, both individually and collectively. Here is another example from the past -

In 1059 the Turkish ruler Sultan Toghrul Beg ravaged the Armenian city of Sebastea, part of the Eastern Roman Empire. Matthew of Edessa wrote this account (c. 1135) of the terrible sufferings of his people -

> "In March 1059 a dreadful disaster befell the Christian faithful. Words cannot express the tribulations they had to suffer; for the Turkish people of Persia, numerous as the sands of the sea, launched attacks against the Christians of Armenia. Many provinces were put to the sword and delivered into slavery by ... men more cruel than wild animals. They advanced on the populous and

noble city of Sebastea, in Armenia, at the head of their black troops, flying their standards, the signs of death. Their roars rolled out like thunder, proclaiming their desire to satisfy their rage.

"On Sunday 6 August 1059 the siege of Sebastea began, as did the slaughter; thousands of corpses littered the ground. What a dreadful scene! The bodies of highly renowned men were piled in a heap as if a forest of trees had been felled, and the ground was soaked with their blood. ... They ruthlessly massacred an immense number of people, carried off a large amount of booty and took untold numbers of captives, men and women, young boys and girls, whom they sold into slavery. ... *(five years later there was another attack)* ...

"(The Turks again) entered the country (and) the inhabitants were put to the sword and driven into slavery ... (They killed) men, women, priests, monks and nobles; the young boys and girls were taken away captive into Persia. ... Frightened out of their wits (the people) started to weep; fathers wept for their sons, sons for fathers, mothers for daughters, daughters for mothers, brothers for brothers, friends for friends. Their situation was desperate and the enemy was all the while redoubling his efforts. Faced with such prolonged attacks the inhabitants resorted to fasting and prayer; their voice rose in unison to God in supplication, begging him, through their tears and sighs, to save them from the savage hordes. ... *(but to little avail, for by 1067 the Turks had thoroughly conquered Armenia and incorporated it into their Islamic empire)* ...

"Who would be strong enough to tell the story of Armenia's plight? Blood flowed everywhere and

> the mountains and hills were trampled underfoot as the hooves of the infidels' horses destroyed them. The smell given off by the dead bodies spread infection far and wide. Persia overflowed with captives; carnivores feasted on corpses. Plunged into mourning and sadness the children of men dissolved into tears because the Creator had turned his gaze far away from them." [42]

Sometimes, of course, our pains are the product of our own actions. Perhaps one of the saddest historical examples of the principle that God seldom rescues people from the consequences of their folly can be found in the story of the 13th century Children's Crusade. Stirred up by popular preachers, tens of thousands of unarmed children, ten to eighteen years old, set off to liberate Jerusalem from the control of the Muslims, expecting by their innocence and faith alone to prevail over the heathen armies. Their fate was both predictable and pitiful. Some were shipwrecked, others perished from hunger, thousands were captured and sold as slaves (by both "Christian" and Muslim marauders); only a small ragged and dispirited remnant managed to struggle back home.

On 29 May 1453 one of the greatest tragedies in Christian history occurred: the ancient and glorious city of Constantinople was overrun by the Turks and sacked. The capital of the Christian Eastern Roman Empire became the capital of a Muslim empire. A city that had been a centre of Christian devotion and learning for a

---

[42] From Chronicles of the Crusades; ed. Elizabeth Hallam; Weidenfeld and Nicolson, London, 1989; pg. 37,40. The territory mentioned (old Armenia) included many towns mentioned in the NT - Antioch, Iconium, Tarsus, etc. The same volume contains numerous other accounts of both individuals and companies of Christians being attacked, pillaged, raped, murdered, by various groups of heathens. One of the individual accounts, for example, tells of a pious abbess who set out on a Christian pilgrimage, but was captured by a group of robbers and raped until she died (pg. 35).

thousand years now became the fulcrum of Islamic culture. In what had once been the richest and most populous part of Christendom the church was reduced to a stifled remnant, which it remains to this day.

Here is a small part of the description of the event written by an observer, a Venetian ship's doctor, Niccolo Barbaro -

> "(The victorious invaders) sought out the convents and all the nuns were taken to the ships and abused and dishonoured by the Turks, and then they were all sold at auction as slaves to be taken to Turkey, and similarly the young women were all dishonoured and sold at auction; some of them preferred to throw themselves into wells and drown.
>
> "These Turks loaded their ships with people and with great treasure ... and for all that day the Turks made a great slaughter of the Christians in the city. Blood flowed on the ground as though it were raining. ... No news could ever be had of the emperor, Constantine XI, or his fate." [43]

Could such things happen again? There is no biblical reason to deny the possibility. Could your home be robbed? Can a Christian woman be attacked and raped? Can Christian children be captured and enslaved? Sadly, such sorrows do fall upon the saints. Despite his promise of protection, the Lord expects us to do whatever we can to protect ourselves, and not to take foolish risks.

---

[43] Ibid. pg. 320,321. The emperor, who was a good and godly man, a firm and just ruler, but helpless against the power of the Turks, in fact died bravely, fighting at the side of the defenders of his city.

Chapter Three:
SUFFERING SAINTS

During the 16th century Marian persecution in England, bishops Hugh Latimer and Nicholas Ridley were burnt at the stake. As the flames sprang up around them, Latimer cried aloud: "Play the man, Master Ridley; we shall this day light such a candle, by God's grace, in England, as I trust shall never be put out." [44]

Yet I wonder if you have even heard the names of those two brave men, let alone have any knowledge of how and why they died? Certainly there are few today, even among devout Christians, who know anything about them. For that very reason the "candle" they lit is flickering low, and its light is dim. As George Santayana said, "Those who cannot remember the past are condemned to repeat it!" [45] Unless then we would find ourselves following our forefathers into the kingdom through rack, scaffold, and stake, we had better remember their sufferings and the reasons for them. That is why every Christian should be aware of the martyrs who gave their all to keep the light of the gospel shining brightly in the world.

We dare not fail them or God by letting that light be extinguished.

---

[44] See Foxe's Book of Martyrs, "History and Martyrdom of Bishop Ridley and Bishop Latimer."

[45] The Life of Reason, Vol. I, ch. xii, "Reason in Common Sense" (dated 1905-1906). Santayana was a Spanish -born American poet, novelist, and philosopher.

Tertullian coined the expression, "The blood of the martyrs is the seed of the church" [46] - out of which a glorious harvest was springing. The same sentiment was echoed 200 years later by Jerome, who himself escaped banishment only by the sudden death of the imperial minister -

> "Recently he sought and obtained a decree of exile against me, and I only wish that he had been able to carry it out ... The church of Christ has been founded by shedding its own blood not that of others, by enduring outrage not by inflicting it. Persecutions have made it grow; martyrdoms have crowned it." [47]

If we fail to nourish that seed of the martyrs by faithfully remembering their heroic deeds, we may well find ourselves adding to it with our own blood.

But let us return to the first Christians, and ask why were they so hated? What drove the imperial authorities to fall with such frenzy upon the nascent church? Here we explore some answers to that question; and our hope is to learn something from the ancient persecutions that may be useful in our own time.

JEWISH PERSECUTIONS

The Book of Acts shows that the first persecutors were the Jews, a situation that continued for as long as the church was thought of as a Jewish sect. During that period the church sought, and usually found, protection from the secular authorities. Christians

---

[46] Apology ch. 50. The saying is preceded by the words, addressed to the Roman authorities: "But go zealously on, (for) you will stand higher with the people if you sacrifice the Christians at their wish. Kill us, torture us, condemn us, grind us to dust; your injustice is the proof that we are innocent. . The more often we are mown down by you, the more in number we grow"

[47] Letter 82;" Post-Nicene Fathers Vol. VI; pg. 174.

recognised the Roman state as a God-given power that made possible the world-wide preaching of the gospel. Hence the state is everywhere spoken of in the NT with respect (with the exception of the Apocalypse) - see Ro 13:1-6; 1 Ti 2:1-3; Tit 3:1; 1 Pe 2:13-17 (notice the command, *"honour the emperor"*); etc. When the church was finally and irreconcilably parted from Judaism, it was no longer susceptible to direct persecution by the Jews and an uneasy peace developed between the now two distinct religions, which still occasionally flared into open hostility.

THE REASONS FOR THE PERSECUTIONS

SECULAR PERSECUTIONS

I have already mentioned that Judaism was an approved religion within the Roman Empire, and Jews were exempted from the duty of burning incense to Caesar. So long as Christianity was seen as a Jewish sect it benefited from those exemptions.

But that situation had begun to change by the end of the first century. The destruction of the Jewish nation brought a complete end to Jewish persecutions of the church, but secular antagonism had begun to grow, until the full power of the state was arrayed against the church, and a determined effort was made to obliterate it. The reasons for that animosity are not always clear, but they probably included the following

CONVENIENT SCAPEGOATS

The Christians were convenient and defenceless scapegoats, whom the population could blame for every tragedy, and upon whom they could vent their fury in the wake of some natural, social, or political disaster

> "The most famous of the early persecutions was that in Rome in A.D. 64, associated with the name of the emperor Nero. Our first detailed account is in the `Annals' of Tacitus ... (who) says that Nero, to meet

> the ugly rumour that a great fire in Rome had been set by his orders, sought to fasten the blame upon the Christians ... Some of the Christians, so Tacitus declares, were wrapped in the hides of wild beasts and were then torn to pieces by dogs. Others, fastened to crosses, were set on fire to illuminate a circus which Nero staged for the crowds in his own gardens ... Tradition, probably reliable, reports that both Peter and Paul suffered death in Rome under Nero ... " [48]

In the pages of literature there is probably no more dramatic description of the horrors endured by the Christians in Rome under the tyranny of Nero than Henryk Sienkiewicz gives in his powerful novel, *Quo Vadis*. [49]

Here is a part of his account. Rows of resin-soaked stakes have been set up, and the Christians bound to them, wreathed with flowers, ivy, and myrtle leaves -

> "Topping the heights, and descending into the hollows, the stakes extended such distances that the nearest looked like ships' masts, and the furthest like a jumble of flower-bedecked thyrsi.
>
> "Soon darkness fell, and the first stars began to shine forth. By the side of every condemned person slaves armed with torches stationed themselves; and

---

[48] Latourette, op. cit., pg 85.

[49] "Quo vadis?" ("Whither goest thou?") is the question Peter is reputed to have asked Jesus, when he met the Master walking toward Rome as the apostle was fleeing from it. Jesus (so legend says) replied: "I am going to Rome to be crucified again." Ashamed, Peter returned to the city and bravely suffered martyrdom for Christ. Sienkiewicz wrote his novel in 1896, and it was translated into English by C. J. Hogarth, and is reprinted from time to time. It contains graphic descriptions of martyrdom in the Roman arena, of Nero illuminating his palace garden party with burning Christians, and of Peter's death by crucifixion upside down.

as soon as a trumpet sounded, as a signal for the spectacle to commence, each slave applied his torch to the base of the stake beside which he was standing.

"Upon this the straw, saturated with oil, which was concealed beneath the garlands blazed up into a flame which, ever-increasing, soon caused the wreaths of ivy to unroll, until the fire had begun to lick the feet of the victims. The spectators remained silent, but from the Gardens there went up one gigantic groan, compounded of thousands of wails of agony. Nevertheless many of the victims, with eyes raised to the star-bespangled heavens, started to sing hymns to the glory of Christ; and as some of the people listened, the hearts of even the most hardened among them contracted for a moment as from the summits of the smaller stakes there came the piteous voices of children crying, `Mother! Mother!' while ruffians in the most advanced stage of intoxication could not repress a shudder at the sight of innocent, childish faces contracted with torture or half-veiled by the smoke which was already suffocating some of the victims." [50]

Similarly, around 150 A.D. the Christians in Ephesus were blamed for a series of earthquakes, and were fiercely harried by the populace. In response to an enquiry, the emperor Marcus Aurelius wrote a letter to the authorities, commanding them to put an end to the persecution unless it could be shown that any Christian was actually working against the state -

"I have no doubt that the gods themselves will expose and punish the guilt of those who blaspheme them. It is in any case more appropriate for the

---

[50] Part III, ch. 21; Heron Books, London; no date; pg. 388, 389.

gods to punish those who refuse to worship them than it is for you to do so. ... (But now) compare your own behaviour with that of the Christians. In times of trouble they become even more cheerful before their God; but during those same times you seem to forget what you should know, and you neglect your duties to the gods and especially to the Immortal. But the Christians, who are steadfast in worship, you banish and hound to death.

"Concerning these Christians, several governors of the provinces once wrote to my divine father, and he replied that they should not be troubled unless they seemed to be acting treasonably against the Roman government. My reply to those who have written to me about how to handle Christians has been the same, to follow the policy of my father." [51]

EASY VICTIMS

Sometimes the persecutions were motivated by sheer greed, which prompted Melito of Sardis (c. 175) to write a letter of protest to the emperor Marcus Aurelius -

" ... for the race of the godly - a thing that never before happened - is now persecuted, being harassed in Asia by recent decrees. For the shameless informers and lovers of other men's goods, taking advantage of the ordinances, plunder openly, day and night pillaging innocent persons ... (Now) if this action is taking place at thy bidding, well and good, ... we, for our part gladly accept the honour of such a death ... But if this decision and

---

[51] Eusebius, Bk 4, ch 13. The authenticity of the letter is doubtful; however, it is still valuable as an illustration of the policy that was indeed followed by a number of the emperors: to avoid actively pursuing Christians, but to punish any who were actual troublemakers.

this fresh ordinance - not fit for use even against barbarian enemies - come not from thee, we beseech thee all the more earnestly not to abandon us to such spoliation at the hands of the people ... "[52]

PRESUMED ATHEISTS

The Christians were accused of being atheists because they had no visible gods, and because they refused to participate in any of the pagan ceremonies. To the profoundly religious peoples of the empire, such apparent atheism was deeply offensive. Religion was interwoven with every facet of Graeco-Roman life, from the highest levels of government to the most intimate acts of the home. Read the poems of Virgil, and you will find them filled with references to the gods and goddesses. Countless religious scenes are carved on the ruins of pagan Rome. Religious rites were mingled with every great civic event, from opening a new building, to celebrating a military victory, to marking the changing seasons, to holding an athletic contest, to sharing a public festival.

Among the Romans religion was conceived as the bond that united the people in loyalty to the state. Piety was an inescapable requirement for both national and personal prosperity. The impious were therefore the enemies of all, and atheists were viewed with horror. The religion of the Romans may not have possessed the personal devotional qualities that we today equate with piety - the Romans felt no need to love their gods - but their religion was nonetheless real to them, and reckoned vital to their wellbeing. Their worship consisted mostly of formal ceremonies, and had little meaning for an individual, it was still deemed indispensable for human welfare. It sustained the life of the state;

---

[52] A New Eusebius; ed. J. Stevenson; SPCK, London, 1975; pg 69-70. The original letter, as quoted by Eusebius, is much longer than the portion I have cited.

it secured the wealth of the city; it preserved the happiness of the family. Inevitably, people who worshipped an invisible God (which to the Romans meant no god at all), and who absolutely refused to honour in any way the state deities, were looked upon with loathing. Notice the cry of the mob in the following account:

> " ... in like manner, they that were condemned to the beasts underwent awful punishments, being stretched on sharp shells and punished with various forms of torture, that, if it were possible, by means of protracted punishment the tyrant might induce them to denial ... (The) right noble Germanicus, by means of his endurance, turned their cowardice into courage. With signal distinction did he fight against the beasts ... in his eagerness to be released the sooner from their unrighteous and lawless mode of life he used force against the wild beast and pulled it on himself. Now it was on this that all the multitude, amazed at the noble conduct of the Godloving and Godfearing race of the Christians, shouted out, `Away with the Atheists!'" [53]

Justin Martyr (c. 150), who gained his honorific from the piety and constancy with which he faced scourging and beheading in Rome, [54] protested against this charge of atheism:

> " ... hence we are called atheists. And we confess that we are atheists, so far as gods of this sort are concerned, but not with respect to the most true God, the Father of righteousness." [55]

---

[53] Ib. pg. 19. the date of the incident was c. 156.
[54] See Foxe's Book of Martyrs; Fleming H. Revell Co, NJ, 1976; pg 18.
[55] Stevenson, op. cit., pg 62, quoting from Justin's first Apology, ch 6.

ENEMIES OF MANKIND

The Christians were accused of being enemies against the human race, because they were so intransigent in their condemnation of many common practices, and because of their refusal to participate in many social, cultural, and religious events. The Roman historian Suetonius, in his *Life of Nero*, says that "punishments were also inflicted upon the Christians, a sect that professed a new and troublesome religious belief."

So Christians seemed to their neighbours to be gloomy separatists, who had withdrawn from society and wished for nothing so much as the early destruction of civilisation. The latter charge was sometimes justified, because of the irresponsible preaching of some who were expecting any day the return of Christ. They gleefully greeted every new earthquake, or flood, or famine, pestilence, or war, as a sure sign of the imminent end of the world. Their ilk are still with us.

The Roman historian Tacitus (55-120) describes Christians as they were commonly viewed in his time -

> "Nero ... punished with the utmost refinement of cruelty <u>a class hated for their abominations</u>, who are commonly called Christians. Christus, from whom their name is derived, was executed at the hands of the procurator Pontius Pilate in the reign of Tiberius. Checked for the moment, this pernicious superstition again broke out, not only in Judea, the source of the evil, but even in Rome. ... Accordingly...an immense multitude was convicted... <u>because of (their) hatred of the human race</u>. Besides being put to death they were made to serve as objects of amusement; they were clad in the hides of beasts and torn to death by dogs; others were crucified, others set on fire to serve to illuminate the night ... All this gave rise to a feeling of pity, <u>even toward men whose guilt merited the</u>

> most exemplary punishment; for it was felt that they were being destroyed not for the public good but to gratify the cruelty of an individual." [56]

Christians were thought to be "haters of the human race" because they were forced by the prevalence of idolatry to withdraw almost entirely from public life. Almost everything that happened in the city was in some way connected with the worship of the gods. Sacrifices were offered at every athletic event, before every play in the theatre, as part of every civic function. There seemed to be no way to avoid some inadvertent participation in pagan worship except to stay away from it all. Those who could not understand this motive easily misjudged and corrupted it. The Fathers frequently refer to such charges and strenuously refute them.

TREASONABLE ACTION

> Christians were accused of treason against the state, because they refused to engage in emperor worship -"Outstanding among the officially supported cults was that of the Emperor. The East had long been familiar with a ruler who was also a divinity. Alexander the Great had been accorded that role. It was natural that Augustus, who had brought peace to the distraught Mediterranean world, should be hailed as an incarnation of divinity. Statues of him were erected and religious ceremonies instituted for him. An imperial cult followed. It might call forth little personal devotion. However, it was regarded as a safeguard of law and order and important for the preservation and prosperity of the realm.

---

[56] "Annales" XV.44; underline mine; Documents of the Christian Church, ed. Henry Bettenson; Oxford University Press, London, 1975; pg. 1,2.

Dissent from it might well be regarded as treasonable and anarchistic." [57]

That became especially true when the pagans heard Christians speaking joyfully about another and greater King, and another and more glorious kingdom. Such language, in that world, could hardly avoid being politically suspect[58]

IMMORAL CANNIBALS

Christians were accused of immorality and of cannibalism, charges that arose from various aspects of Christian behaviour:

- the custom of admitting only fully initiated people to the eucharist, which led to garbled reports about Christians eating "flesh" and drinking "blood", practising cannibalism and incest;
- the covert manner in which (because of persecution) they were often compelled to meet, which led to wild speculation about what they did in their secret gatherings;
- the open welcome into the church given to women as well as to men, which seemed scandalous to a society more familiar with, say, the popular "mystery" religions, which admitted only men);

---

[57] Latourette, op. cit., pg 23,24.

[58] Remember also that in the ancient world, as still in many lands today, there was a strong union between religion and state. The idea of a complete separation between church and state is quite modern, and even now holds sway in only a few countries. Throughout most of history, and in most countries, the fortunes of the state and its deities were thought to be deeply intertwined. To destroy a state usually entailed also the destruction of its gods, or at least their subjugation beneath the stronger deity of the conqueror. But then the reverse was also thought to be true: destroy its religion and you inevitably also break the strength of the state.

- the warm love Christians were known to offer other Christians, even those with whom they had scanty acquaintance, which led to suspicions of lewd intimacy;
- the practice of calling each other "brother" and "sister", which many interpreted as a sign of homosexual conduct.

Note that the mutual love, which was and still is the chief glory of the church, was a source of scorn to the pagan world. Thus Tertullian wrote -

> " ... it is mainly the deeds of love so noble that lead many to put a brand upon us. *`See,'* they say, *`how they love one another,'* for themselves are animated by mutual hatred ... And they are wrath with us too, because we call each other brethren ... " [59]

TERTULLIAN AND AUGUSTINE

SOCIAL COLLAPSE

In the face of a deteriorating political and economic order, the church, separate, stern, austere, and (to the pagan mind) mysterious, seemed to be a cause of the weakness that was overtaking the empire.

It was argued that the gods that had made Rome great were now being neglected, and were no longer protecting the empire; indeed every disorder was blamed on the Christian "atheists".

> "In the middle of the third century ... Rome celebrated the thousandth anniversary of her founding, and looked back to the days of prosperity, stability, and unquestioned authority in the Mediterranean world. How the gods had favoured

---

[59] Apology, ch 39. See also the similar complaint expressed at least two centuries earlier by a Jewish writer in the Wisdom of Solomon (2:1-22), which is quoted at the end of Chapter Five below.

her! Now the foundations of the economic, political, and social structure were crumbling. Public calamities such as earthquakes and pestilences abounded. Barbarians hovered on the frontiers.

> "A superstitious populace was easily persuaded that the gods were angry because so many Christians had left the old faith." [60]

There was also just the simple and common human fear of change, of seeing the familiar destroyed, and something unknown taking over. A similar kind of reaction is developing in some parts of our own society, where communities that have never known any religious presence except Christianity, suddenly find mosques, temples, and synagogues standing where once only the church stood. Many people do not know how to handle this, and there are always some who can find no other way to respond than violence. In the case of the Roman world, there was good reason for its apprehensions -

> "Crude and misinformed though some of the criticisms of Christianity were, there was an awareness that a force was entering the world which, if given free scope would overturn the existing culture. Dimly, to be sure, and imperfectly, but with an appreciation of the actualities, non-Christians sensed that because of its revolutionary nature, its uncompromising character, and its claim to the allegiance of all mankind, Christianity was more to be feared by the established order than any of its many competitors, not even excepting Judaism." [61]

---

[60] Howard F. Vos, Beginnings in Church History; Moody Bible Institute, 1977; pg. 33.

[61] Latourette, op. cit., pg 82.

Against the absurd idea that Christians were to blame for the present disasters, all the apologists raised a vigorous protest. Here is one sample from Tertullian:

> "If the Tiber rises as high as the city walls, if the Nile does not send its waters up over the fields, if the heavens give no rain, if there is an earthquake, if there is famine or pestilence, straightway the cry is, `Away with the Christians to the lion!' ... Pray, tell me, how many calamities befell the world ... before the coming ... of Christ? ... But where - I do not say were Christians, those despisers of your gods - but where were your gods themselves in those days? ... "[62]

Tertullian then gives a long list of pre-Christian disasters, mixed in with a powerful, sarcastic, and passionate argument concerning the providence and government of the God of heaven, in contrast with the imbecilities endemic in pagan idolatry.

Several long passages in Augustine's remarkable *City of God* (completed in 426), present the same idea, and demonstrate the lunacy of blaming Christians for the perils that were coming upon the empire. He introduces the issue in this way -

> "My purpose now is to proceed to treat of the disasters which Rome has suffered since its foundation, whether at home or in the subject provinces, disasters which they would blame on the Christian religion, if at that time the teaching of the gospel had rung out with its sweeping condemnation of their false deceiving gods. You must bear in mind that in mentioning these facts I

---

[62] Apology, ch. 40. "Lion" in the singular is correct. Tertullian himself mocks the absurdity of the cry ("What? Will you throw so many to only one beast?"); but its aphoristic form shows how often the cry must have been repeated.

am still dealing with the ignorant, the people whose stupidity has given rise to the popular proverb, `No rain! It's all the fault of the Christians!' ...

"(So they) support the vulgar notion that the disasters which are bound to fall on humanity during a given period and over a given area are to be laid at the door of Christianity. ...

"So let us help them to recall the many and various disasters which overwhelmed the Roman State before Christ's incarnation - before his name became known to the nations, and received that honour which arouses their ineffectual envy. And in the face of these facts let them defend their gods if they can, assuming that the gods are worshipped in order that the worshippers may escape such calamities. For if they suffer anything of this kind now, they contend that we are to be held responsible. Why then did the gods allow the catastrophes which I am going to mention to fall upon their worshippers, before the proclamation of Christ's name offended them and before Christ's name put a stop to their sacrifices?" [63]

Augustine then details the many moral, political, fiscal, and natural disasters that had frequently ravaged Rome in the years before Christ was even born. He wrote from a theological and philosophical viewpoint; but another famous work, by Paulus Orosius (c. 385 - c. 420), tackled the same theme from an historical perspective (his book was popular for centuries as a Christian apology and historical text book, and it was translated into English by Alfred the Great [849-899].)

---

[63] Book II, ch. 2 & 3; tr. by Henry Bettenson; Penguin Books, London, 1977; pg. 50.

So much for the causes of the persecutions. The next chapter examines the actual persecutions; but before turning to it, let us look just once more at the question of why the gospel was so unappealing to many sincere pagans. Robert Browning, in his poem *Cleon*, describes a discussion by letter between a fictitious monarch, King Protus, and his equally mythical friend Cleon, who was a philosopher, artist, and poet. Protus was troubled about the question of life after death, and he wrote that if philosophy could not ease his dread of the grave, then Cleon should send the king's letter on to that new teacher, the apostle Paul.

Cleon decried the king's willingness to turn to the Christian religion -

> I cannot tell thy messenger aright
>
> Where to deliver what he bears of thine
>
> To one called Paulus - we have heard his fame;
>
> Indeed, if Christus be not one with him -
>
> I know not, nor am troubled much to know.
>
> Thou canst not think a mere barbarian Jew,
>
> As Paulus proves to be, one circumcised,
>
> Hath access to a secret shut from us?
>
> Thou wrongest our philosophy, O king,
>
> In stooping to enquire of such an one,
>
> As if his answer could impose at all.
>
> He writeth, doth he? well, and he may write.
>
> Oh, the Jew findeth scholars! certain slaves
>
> Who touched on this same isle, preached him and Christ;

> And (as I gathered from a bystander)
>
> Their doctrines could be held by no sane man.[64]

Yet those same doctrines routed all the ancient speculations, and went on to become the most powerful force in human history.

---

[64] "Cleon" by Robert Browning (1812-1889)

Chapter Four:
THE TWO GREAT PERIODS OF PERSECUTION

CHRISTIANS COURAGEOUS

> The lopped tree in time may grow again,
> Most naked plants renew both fruit and flower;
> The sorriest wight may find release of pain,
> The driest soil suck in some moistening shower;
> Times go by turns, and chances change by course,
> From foul to fair, from better hap to worse. [65]

Times do indeed "go by turns", and for the church tend to flow from persecution to prosperity and back again. In this chapter we explore the changing fortunes of the church in its relationships with imperial Rome. Commonly (following the pattern of Foxe's Book of Martyrs [66], it is said that the church suffered ten periods of persecution prior to the collapse of the western empire at the end of the 5th century. More simply, there were two main, and rather different, periods of persecution -

---

[65] Times Go By Turns, first stanza; Robert Southwell (1561?-1595), English poet and Jesuit priest and martyr. He was accused of high treason (for holding to the Roman Catholic faith), thrown into the Tower, tortured, and on February 21, 1595, hanged, drawn, and quartered at Tyburn. He was beatified in 1929.

[66] John Foxe (1516-1587) was an Englishman who converted from the Roman Catholic faith to the principles of the Reformation. He became an Anglican priest and martyrologist. His famous book (published in 1563) tells the stories of Christian martyrs from the early church until the 16th century. It is still in print.

LOCAL AND SPASMODIC - *A.D. 64 - 250*

Persecution prior to the middle of the third century was mostly local, and spasmodic, provoked primarily by neighbourhood jealousies, fears, or conflict. Local authorities rather than the imperial government were its usual instigators. Those who were victims of the persecutors' violence found it terrible enough, but the loss of life was comparatively small, and it had little effect upon the church at large.

This is highlighted by remembering that across the first three centuries of this era some 54 emperors ruled, but scarcely more than a dozen of them actively harmed the church. Indeed, on several occasions the imperial government actually intervened either to stop, or at least to lessen, the sufferings of the church. For example, here are two policy declarations, the first from the emperor Trajan (c. 112), and the second from Hadrian (c. 124) -

> "You have taken the right line, my dear Pliny, in examining the cases of those denounced to you as Christians ... (My rule is that) they are not to be sought out. If they are informed against and the charge is proved, then they must of course be punished. But with this reservation: if anyone denies that he is a Christian, and actually proves it - that is, by worshipping our gods - he shall be pardoned as a result of his recantation, however suspect he may have been with respect to the past." [67]

---

[67] Adapted from Bettenson, op. cit. pg. 4. Pliny was a Roman governor who had written to Trajan for advice on how to handle the Christians, since there were so many of them, who mostly seemed to be law-abiding citizens.

So despite common opinion, the number of Christian martyrs prior to the year 250 was not high. This is confirmed by the clear statement of Origen (c. 240) -

> "But with regard to the Christians, because they were taught not to avenge themselves upon their enemies (and thus have observed laws of a mild and philanthropic character); and because they would not, although able, have made war even if they had received authority to do so, - they have obtained this reward from God, that he has always warred in their behalf, and on certain occasions has restrained those who rose up against them and desired to destroy them. For in order to remind others, that by seeing a *few* engaged in a struggle for their religion, they also might be better fitted to despise death, some, on special occasions, and these individuals who can be easily numbered, have endured death for the sake of Christianity, - God not permitting the whole nation to be exterminated, but desiring that it should continue, and that the whole world should be filled with this salutary and religious doctrine."[68]

Indeed, it has been said that more people have died for Christ in the latter half of our 20th century than were martyred in the first 300 years. According to one authority, in the year 1990 alone at least 250,000 people perished because they were Christians.[69] That violence has not ceased, and there are still many parts of the world where men and women who openly confess Christ place their lives in jeopardy.

---

[68] Contra Celsus III.8; Ante-Nicene Fathers, Vol. 4, pg 467,468. Notice the expressions "few", and "easily number

[69] A figure calculated by church statistician David Barrett, of the World Evangelisation Research Centre

The persecution faced by the early church, then, did not hinder its growth, but rather strengthened it. Enough people suffered to deter easy conversions and to keep the church alert and pure; but the great majority of Christians lived without peril or harm.

The church leaders also acted wisely, and prevented much harm by discouraging the urge for martyrdom. Wherever possible, people at risk of persecution were encouraged to flee, and to return to their homes only after the fury had abated. Those who deliberately sought martyrdom were rebuked.

Tens of thousands heeded the advice of their pastors, and escaped before they could be arrested. Many of them lost all their possessions, but their lives, and those of their families, were preserved, and their witness for Christ was able to continue.

But there was a second and more terrible period of persecution, one that was -

UNIVERSAL AND CONTINUOUS - *A.D. 250 - 324*

DECIUS

In the year 249, the emperor Decius, faced with the threatened disintegration of the empire, resolved to unite it once again around the old Roman virtues and religion. His hope was to restore the empire to the glory it had enjoyed under Augustus. He decided that the best way to begin achieving this goal was to require all the subject peoples to emulate in their own localities the great religious sacrifice that he would offer to the empire's guardian deities in Rome.

No one was required to abandon his or her personal religion, but edicts were issued that commanded all citizens to sacrifice to the state gods, and specifically to burn incense to the divinity of Caesar. Those who obeyed the injunction were given a certificate, called a *libellus* ("little book", or "pamphlet"), of which some 40 copies are still extant. Anyone who lacked a *libellus* was guilty of the capital offence of treason against the state.

In practice, a citizen had to do no more than burn a pinch of incense in the presence of a government official, and say, '*Caesar is Lord.*' But for many devout people even that simple act was too close to idolatry, and they braved awful tortures and death rather than yield. However, there were many others who circumvented the law by purchasing a *libellus* from a venal official; and many apostasised under the threat of terrible pain.

Still, enough Christians defied the imperial edict to persuade Decius that the church was undermining the morale of the entire empire, so he set himself to destroy it. He saw it as the main obstacle he faced in his quest to rebuild national coherence and strength. A new set of edicts was promulgated, demanding the obliteration of Christianity.

This was the first truly empire-wide persecution, and the first serious attempt by a monarch to destroy systematically the very fabric of the church. For the first time also there was wide compliance by government officials with the imperial decree. The appointed commissioners made strenuous efforts to ensure that every citizen had either obtained a libellus, or else was arrested and punished for sedition.

Under this renewed onslaught, the number of those who fell away (which included even bishops) produced a crisis in the church, and joy to its enemies. The crisis was heightened by the bitter schisms that occurred. Some reckoned that there was little harm - for the sake of national unity and peace for the church - in burning a pinch of incense. They refused to allow that they had been guilty of idolatry, and saw no reason why they should be punished by sterner Christians for acknowledging that Caesar was lord.

Others, when the persecution had run its course, fiercely opposed allowing those who had lapsed to come back into the church. Some were willing to restore the backsliders, but quarrelled about how they should be restored, and what penalty or discipline should be exacted from them. Some of the divisions that arose from those arguments continued for centuries. Nor was the debate altogether solved. There is still tension today between those who see the church as a holy and discrete group of dedicated saints, and those who see it as a harbour for hurting and broken sinners. The war goes on (albeit more gently than in the past) between those who want to purge the church of all baleful influence, and those who are content for wheat and tares to grow together until the day of final harvest.

Fortunately, Decius was killed in battle only two years after his edict, and his successor (Gallus) vas too much occupied with other troubles to give much attention to fulfilling the Decian decrees. Thus the severity of the persecution was abated. But had Decius lived, he might have succeeded, for later history showed that the church was not immune from destruction. It has been obliged (as we shall see) to hand over to other faiths lands that were once wholly Christian.

One of the victims of the Decian persecution was Origen, who was among the greatest teachers of the early church. Here is his story, which begins in the year 202, when he was 17 years of age. He was the son of wealthy Christian parents, and was himself a devout and zealous young man. A persecution had broken out, at the instigation of the emperor Septimius Severus, and Origen's father Leonidas had been arrested. Eusebius gives this account -

> "As the flame of persecution had been kindled greatly, and multitudes had gained the crown of martyrdom, such desire for martyrdom seized the soul of Origen, although yet a boy, that he went close to danger, springing forward and rushing to the conflict in his eagerness ... (But God) prevented his desire through the agency of his mother. For at first, entreating him, she begged him to have compassion on her motherly feelings toward him; but finding, that when he had learned that his father had been seized and imprisoned, he was set more resolutely and completely carried away with his zeal for martyrdom, she hid all his clothing, and

> thus compelled him to remain at home. But as there was nothing else that he could do, and his zeal beyond his age would not suffer him to be quiet, he sent to his father an encouraging letter on martyrdom, in which he exhorted him, saying, 'Take heed not to change your mind on our account.'"

The young man apparently found the prospect of rushing naked through the streets far more daunting than a terrible death in the arena! So he was denied his wish for martyrdom. His father was cruelly put to death, and all of the family's possessions were confiscated.

So from a position of considerable affluence the family was reduced to abject poverty, and Origen had to assume responsibility for caring for his mother and six younger brothers. This adversity, far from discouraging him, inflamed his zeal all the more, and he laboured mightily, studying and then teaching Greek philology and literature, and copying manuscripts. His efforts were rewarded, and he eventually restored the family's prosperity. However, he continued to live very abstemiously himself; indeed, so great was his urge toward holiness, and his desire to serve Christ alone, while he was still a young man (about 25 years old) he acted literally on Mt 19:12, took a knife and castrated himself - an act of youthful folly that he later ruefully denounced.

He mastered philosophy, theology, and other disciplines and became one of the first great Bible commentators, and perhaps the first of the early teachers to produce a systematic statement of all the major doctrines of Christianity. He established a flourishing seminary that became the greatest theological school of its time. It remains the progenitor and model of every Bible college that has since been built. Origen himself provides a fine example of the godliness, the discipline, the love of learning, that should mark all who wish to be noble teachers of the Word of life.

In the end, after some 55 years of devoted service to Christ, the great man gained the prize he had sought as a youth - a martyr's crown. During the Decian persecution Origen was arrested, put in chains, tortured, burdened with a crushing iron collar, and racked over a long period.

Eusebius describes his sufferings -

> " ... how many things he endured for the word of Christ, bonds and bodily tortures and torments under the iron collar and in the dungeon; and for how many days with his feet stretched four spaces in the stocks he bore patiently the threats of fire and whatever other things were inflicted by his enemies ... as his judge strove eagerly with all his might not to end his life."[70]

Throughout the agonies of prolonged and repeated torture, Origen remained steadfast in his faith. His tormentors, since they could not break his spirit, finally released him; but his health was ruined and he soon died, shattered in body, but still mighty in spirit.

VALERIAN

The persecution begun by Decius was continued with varying severity for nearly ten years by the new emperor Valerian.[71] His policy was not motivated by any personal hatred of Christians, but again by a desire to strengthen the empire against its foes, which at that time were many. Valerian found that he had inherited an empire that was on the edge of ruin. Plague was rampaging in many places, invaders were penetrating the northern and eastern boundaries, within the empire there was considerable civil strife, seditions, and threatened revolt. So, like his predecessor, Valerian

---

[70] Bk 6, ch 39.

[71] The emperor Gallus, who reigned less than 3 years, intervened between Decius and Valerian, but he neither promulgated nor withdrew the Decian decrees.

resolved to secure heaven's favour by uniting all the people in a common act of sacrifice.

One sad aspect of these persecutions is that Rome's policy had always been one of religious toleration. She was content to allow each community to worship whatever god it pleased, so long as the people accepted also the overarching "imperial cult", which honoured the divine spirit that was thought to be resident in the emperors. This cult gave reverence to the highest deities in the Roman pantheon, those whose favour was believed to have made the empire great. It required no personal devotion toward the Roman gods, simply an occasional act of formal respect.

Within the general policy of religious freedom, most people found no problem in adding the Roman state religion to their local cult, and burning a pinch of incense from time to time as part of their civic duty. But for the Christians it was impossible. Inevitably, they were viewed as public enemies, disturbers of the peace, traitors, a peril to everyone's safety.

By this time, the church had already recovered from the Decian troubles, and had also gained a much tougher temper. Most Christians refused to obey Valerian's edict. The number of protesters eventually became so large that around 258 the emperor's patience snapped, and he unleashed a violent terror upon the church. He shrewdly decided to concentrate (for the first time) upon its leaders, reckoning that their destruction would lead to the ruin of the church itself. So he ordered that bishops, priests, and deacons be executed, church properties confiscated, and public officials who were Christians be enslaved.

For example, in 258 Cyprian, bishop of Carthage, was charged by the proconsul Galerius Maximus -

> "You have long lived an irreligious life, and have drawn together a number of men bound by an unlawful association, and professed yourself an open enemy to the gods and religion of Rome ... (Whereas) therefore you have been apprehended as

principal and ringleader in these infamous crimes, you shall be made an example to those whom you have wickedly associated with you; the authority of law shall be ratified in your blood."[72]

The devastation was appalling, and had the persecution continued the church may well have suffered a blow from which it might not have been able to recover. But once again providence intervened. Only two years after issuing his edict Valerian was captured by the Persians (in 260). This was the first time that a Roman emperor had been captured in battle, and it sent a shock of horror and shame from end to end of the empire. The Persians would accept no ransom, and Valerian died in chains. Many people saw it as a judgment of God upon a persecuting prince. The violence came to an end, and for 40 years the church had peace, suffering only sporadic and local harassment.

DIOCLETIAN

In 303 began the bitterest trial the church had yet faced, when Diocletian set himself once and for all to annihilate Christianity. At first he was reluctant to embark upon a pogrom of the church, but he was finally incited to it by his junior colleague Galerius, whose motive was again not so much religious antipathy as a conservative desire to restore Rome to its old virtues, disciplines, and institutions. But this necessarily involved honouring the Roman gods through various public rites, which Christians could not in good conscience perform. So when the Christians resisted, Diocletian issued various edicts, commanding the destruction or appropriation of churches. He too designed first to destroy the clergy, and then the lay leaders of the churches, and eventually, when that failed, he determined upon the complete extermination of Christianity.

---

[72] A New Eusebius, ed. J. Stevenson; S.P.C.K., London, 1975; pg. 261. Cyprian was condemned and at once beheaded

Eusebius, in Books 8 & 9 of his *Church History*, provides a gripping account of this last battle in the warfare between imperial Rome and the church. The heroism of the martyrs, young and old, men and women, was extraordinary. Every imaginable barbarity was practised upon them, but they remained resolute. Among others, the first known British martyrdom occurred during this last great struggle. The story is told by Foxe

"Alban was the first British martyr. This man was a pagan, but being of a humane disposition, he sheltered an English ecclesiastic name Amphibalus, whom some officers were in pursuit of on account of his religion. The example and discourses of the refugee made a great impression on the mind of Alban; he longed to become a member of a religion which charmed him; the fugitive minister, happy in the opportunity, took great pains to instruct him, and, before his discovery, perfected Alban's conversion. ... (Alban helped Amphibalus to escape, was arrested in his stead, carried before the Roman governor, and commanded) to sacrifice to the pagan deities. Alban declared that he would not comply and professed himself to be a Christian. The governor ordered him to be scourged, but he bore the punishment with great fortitude, and he seemed to acquire new resolution from his sufferings: he was then beheaded."[73]

Despite the violence and wide extent of this last great imperial persecution the church was saved from ruin for two reasons:

---

[73] cit., pg 25,26.

> *first*: in various parts of the empire the authorities were displeased by the edicts and desultory in fulfilling them.

The Christians were now numerous, with many of them wealthy and influential, and peace had endured for decades. Many officials thought it folly to tear the community apart by embarking upon a religious war against their own people.

> *second*, Diocletian's health collapsed, which led to his abdication only two years later (305).

On this matter, the historian and apologist Lactantius wrote a memorable account of the violent deaths that one after the other struck down persecuting emperors.[74] The same idea, that the prayers of the church finally prevailed over all its enemies, either to change them or to overthrow them, was presented by Origen -

> "We do, when occasion requires, give help to kings, and that, so to say, a divine help, `putting on the whole armour of God.' And this we do in obedience to the injunction of the apostle, `*I exhort, therefore, that first of all, supplications, prayers, intercessions, and giving of thanks, be made for all men; for kings, and for all that are in authority;*' and the more anyone excels in piety, the more effective help does he render to kings, even more than is given by soldiers, who go forth and slay as many of the enemy as they can ... And as we by our prayers vanquish all demons who stir up war, and lead to the violation of oaths, and disturb the peace, we in this way are much more helpful to the king than those who go into the field and fight for them ... And none fight better for the king than we do ... (for) we fight on his behalf, forming a special army

---

[74] "On the Manner in which the Persecutors Died," Ante-Nicene Fathers, Vol VII; pg. 301 ff.

- an army of piety - by offering our prayers to God."[75]

THE END OF PERSECUTION

A civil war broke out following Diocletian's abdication, which brought persecution in the west virtually to an end - although it continued in the east (especially in Palestine and Egypt). Finally Constantine, after defeating all his rivals, united the whole empire under his rule and the days of suffering came to an end. Indeed, even before his power was fully consolidated he had joined with Licinius in issuing a policy of full toleration of all religions. This was the famous *Edict of Milan* (issued in 313), which read in part -

> "Of all the things that are beneficial to mankind, the worship of God must stand highest and be our foremost concern. Therefore it is right that Christians and all peoples be allowed freedom to observe whichever religious belief they choose. The God who rules in heaven will then look upon us, and upon all the peoples over whom we rule, with favour. We therefore decree that all ... who choose the Christian religion may freely continue in its observance. Let no one prohibit or hinder them; let no one molest or injure them. Furthermore, this decree applies to all religions. Every person is granted the right to practise their religion without interference. This agrees with the good order of the empire, and will promote the present public wellbeing, that every person should be free to worship God in his own way ... "[76]

---

[75] "Against Celsus", Bk 8, ch 73. Written c. 245. Ante-Nicene Fathers, Vol IV.

[76] Lactantius, "On the Death of the Persecutors" XLVIII. The decree was issued jointly by Constantine and Licinius.

Notice that the Edict of Milan did not, as many have supposed, make Christianity the state religion of the empire, but simply declared that all people, including Christians, were to be allowed full freedom of worship. Probably less than half of the population was yet Christian. But beginning with Constantine, the succession of Christian emperors bestowed on the church more and more favour, and paganism fell into rapid decline. So, with the church waxing ever mightier, the long era of persecution came to an end. We might say, though, that its true, and sad, climax did not actually come until a hundred years after Constantine, when late in the 4th century the emperor Theodosius the Great made Christianity the state religion. All other religions were proscribed, and the church began to persecute the pagans, whose gods were now banned by law. Outwardly at least Christianity had triumphed.

CONCLUSION

The stories of the persecutions are not just gory and tragic footnotes to history. Although other religions were sometimes persecuted by the Roman state, none had to endure such prolonged and relentless suffering as did the church. But this raises a question: *how did the church, which began in such obscurity, and which had such overwhelming strength arraigned against it, manage to defeat all its foes?*

Not only that: the church at the same time developed an organisation second only to that of the empire; forced the state to capitulate and to honour it; became the sole lawful religion of the state; and then outgrew and outlived the very power that had striven so viciously to destroy it!

Some of the reasons for this astonishing success were -

> ➢ By the time any serious attempt was made to purge the empire of Christianity the number of Christians was already too high. In some parts of north Africa by the middle third century they were in the majority; and elsewhere they were at least a substantial minority that reached into all levels of

society. The social cost of trying to eradicate them was simply unbearable. Few government officials made any consistent attempt to implement the imperial order to destroy the church. Nor was it difficult to bribe other officials to make only a token show of oppressing their Christian neighbours. The influence of the church itself had made the barbarity of the torture chamber increasingly distasteful to thoughtful people. So although the last three empire-wide persecutions were fierce - and had they continued would have wreaked enormous harm - in the event their short duration and their imperfect performance made them ineffective.

- ➢ The church swiftly recovered all that it had lost, and more, and emerged stronger than ever.

- ➢ The Christian apologists had reached a point of development where they could present theology at the highest level, and with a competence equal to the finest of the classical scholars. Their polemics against idolatry, exposing the folly of the pagan beliefs, were finally unanswerable. One by one the pagan philosophers had to abandon the field and leave the Christians alone in possession of the intellectual territory. Christians could be killed; but their ideas were immortal.

- ➢ Good people among the pagans were appalled at the cruelties being perpetrated in the name of their gods, and began to wonder how such gods could merit worship. Associated with this, the bravery of the martyrs raised the inevitable question of why people would die so cheerfully for Christ? The cavil that they were fanatical idiots could not survive personal observation of the happy, prosperous, and peaceful lives enjoyed by Christian families. They were known to be honest in all their dealings, gentle in their relationships, respectful to all, diligent in work - in a word, excellent neighbours, workers, and civil servants. Under the fear of war or natural disaster, or under threat from the authorities, pagans could for a time be aroused against the Christians; but in the end common sense would prevail, and community resistance to persecution grew ever stronger.

Yet after examining various reasons for the triumph of the early church over every enemy and every competitor, Latourette dismisses them all but one. About that one reason he says -

> "The more one examines into the various factors which seem to account for the extraordinary victory of Christianity the more one is driven to search for a cause which underlies them. It is clear that from the very beginning of Christianity there must have occurred a vast release of energy, unequalled in the history of the race. Without it the future course of the faith is inexplicable."

> That burst of energy was ascribed by the early disciples to the Founder of their faith. "Something happened to the men who associated with Jesus. In his contact with them, in his crucifixion and in their assurance of his resurrection and of the continued living presence with his disciples of his Spirit, is to be found the major cause of the success of Christianity ... Without Jesus, Christianity would not have sprung into existence, and from him and beliefs about him came its main dynamic."[77]

---

[77] A History of Christianity (in 5 vols); Vol 1, "The First Five Centuries," ch 4, pg 167,168; Zondervan Pub. House.

Chapter Five:
CATHOLIC CHURCHES

Amid his coarseness and brutality, Henry VIII of England had at least one virtue - a nice impartiality on matters of religion. Since he had no personal religious scruples, he could look with equal disdain upon both Catholic and Protestant zealots. On one occasion he burned to death three Protestants, and three Catholics, all for practising their religion in a way that offended the king! On another occasion "he had a representative of each faction tied to the same stake, where they continued until the flames consumed them to preach their opposing doctrines with undiminished fervour." [78]

However, those unhappy quarrels had begun many centuries before King Henry offered his rough demonstration of impartiality. Which brings us to a point in our history where we begin to look at some of the things that have often divided Christians -

GOVERNMENT

THE THREE MAJOR FORMS OF CHURCH GOVERNMENT

VARIOUS CHOICES

Across the centuries, three different kinds of government have been practised in various parts of the church:

> ➢ episcopal - rule by a bishop

---

[78] From the "Introduction" by John Moore to W. H. Ainsworth's novel, Windsor Castle; Heron Books, London; undated.

- presbyterian - rule by the elders
- congregational - rule by the people

The proponents of those three forms have often argued that theirs is the only one sanctioned by God, and they seek proof either from scripture or from tradition, or both.

Unhappily for those who favour either presbyterian or congregational government, neither scripture nor tradition offer much consolation. Biblical support for those forms is sparse, and they have no strong tradition reaching further back than the Reformation (that is, the 16th century).

That does not give episcopalians any reason to boast. They too lack any substantive biblical support - although they may claim that at least tradition is on their side, for episcopal rule over the churches was fairly well established by the middle of the second century.

The unfortunate fact is that neither the NT nor the writings of the first 100 years offer any definitive evidence about how the early church was structured. At best we may say that by the year 100 the following offices were usual:

THE THREE LEVELS OF MINISTRY

- deacons (who included women in at least some of the churches)
- elders (synonymous with presbyters, overseers, and the like)
- bishops (often synonymous with elders, but there is some evidence that bishops held a higher authority)

But even if bishops were given a higher status, they were still local church functionaries, more akin to the modern idea of a pastor than to that of a modern bishop. Even in the local church the bishop did not always have the sole authority given to a pastor today. Many churches apparently had a plural bishopric (cp. Ph 1:1).

THE RISE OF THE MONARCHICAL BISHOPRIC

However, by the middle of the 2nd century (that is, by 150), while no fixed structure had yet been adopted by, nor imposed upon, all the churches, there is evidence that the idea of a monarchical bishopric was beginning to prevail. The bishop was now readily accepted as the prime leader of a local church, and in some cases appears to have had authority over a cluster of churches. Thus Ignatius, in his letters to eight churches, argues vigorously for the senior role of the bishop, and distinguishes him from presbyters and deacons. He leaves an impression that there was only one bishop to a city, along with several congregations, each with its own presbyters and deacons.

Yet the very energy of Ignatius' pleas seems to indicate considerable opposition to his ideas. We are left with the suspicion that the notion of a ruling bishop was not yet firmly entrenched in the minds of the believers!

"(Your deacons) are subject to the bishop as they are to the grace of God, and they submit to the presbytery as they do to the law of Christ ... It is right that you should not be too familiar with your bishop just because he is young, but you should offer him all honour, remembering the power of God the Father ... Let there be no pretence in your submission to your bishop, out of reverence for Christ who has commanded us to show obedience. Anyone who tries to deceive the bishop who is visible in the end succeeds only in mocking the bishop who is invisible ... So let nothing arise among you that might divide you, but stay united around your bishop and with those who have been given rule over you ... For so long as you are subject to the bishop as if to Jesus Christ you will no longer be living like ordinary men, but rather after the pattern of Christ, who gave his life for us ... This is my rule, which you are already following, that you should do nothing without the bishop ... (Yes), let all of you reverence the bishop as you would Jesus Christ, who is the Son of the Father, and treat the presbyters like the sanhedrin of God, like the assembly of the apostles. Where these are not present, there is no church. ... (You must) continue in intimate union with Jesus Christ our God, and with the bishop ... Anyone who does anything apart from the bishop, the presbytery, and the deacons is a person who lacks a good conscience. ... Make sure that no one does anything connected with the church without the bishop. The only true and fitting eucharist is one that is administered either by the bishop or by one to whom the task has been delegated. ... It is unlawful, without the bishop, for anyone to baptise, or to celebrate a love-feast ... "[79]

Note also that Ignatius commonly refers to "the bishop (singular) -

"I greet your bishop, who is truly worthy of God, and your presbyters, who grace the name of God, and your deacons, who are fellow-servants with me of Christ."[80]

What is perhaps even more surprising is the surprisingly high level of authority Ignatius gives to the bishop

"Your bishop stands in the stead of God, and your presbyters occupy the place of the apostles, while your deacons ... have been entrusted with the service of Jesus Christ. ... As therefore the Lord did nothing, either by himself or by the apostles, without the Father, because he was united with him, so neither should you do anything without your bishop and presbyters."[81]

It is easy to imagine how furiously those exalted claims must have been disputed by more democratically minded souls!

One sad development[82] is the suggestion that lies in the words of Ignatius that in the mid-second century church the governmental office of bishop or presbyter had already replaced the charismatic office of the apostle and/or prophet.

---

[79] See Mag 2,3; Tral 2,3,7; Smyrna 8; plus many other references in his letters.

[80] See Smyrna 12.

[81] See Mag 6,7.

[82] A phrase that I suppose reveals my own prejudice!

The arguments of such Fathers as Ignatius soon prevailed, so that by the end of the 2nd century the monarchical bishopric was becoming firmly established throughout the church. At the same time, the church in Rome had begun to gain a certain pre-eminence. Indeed, the custom can already be observed of disputes being referred, not to Jerusalem (as happened in Acts), but to Rome.

That process continued until, by the end of the 5th century, with the church now established by law, and the whole empire at least nominally Christian, a wide gulf had developed between clergy and laity, and between ordinary priests and their bishops. The idea was now established that bishops were necessary for the very existence of the church. Some went so far as to argue that they were the church, for nothing could be done without their approval. Where there was a bishop, there was the church; where there was no bishop, there was no church.

DISSENTING VOICES

That accumulation of power by the bishops did not happen without strong dissent. At all times there were groups of people who resisted the establishment of an episcopal hierarchy, arguing instead for the autonomy of the local church. Such dissenters were rejected as heretics by the Catholic[83] church (as the majority group now called itself). There were also other groups of churches who considered themselves part of the Catholic church, but refused to allow that the bishop of Rome had any primacy over them. The church at the end of the 5th century was not yet "Roman" Catholic. Another 100 years were to pass before the western churches would become subservient to the bishop of Rome. In the east the bishops and pastors never did allow the pope supremacy over them.

---

[83] The word simply means "universal", that is "world-wide".

There were also, at various times, large clusters of churches in various parts of the empire, and beyond its borders, who altogether separated themselves from the Catholic church; for example -

THE MONTANISTS

Montanus was a mid-second century prophet who preached the nearness of Christ's return and believed that he had a commission from God to restore the charismata to the church. Glossolalia was practised, prophesying was encouraged, along with an attempt to recapture the healing ministry described in the Acts of the Apostles. Montanism expanded rapidly, especially in North Africa and Asia Minor, and for a time was the majority group in those areas. Its most renowned convert was the brilliant lawyer, apologist, and theologian Tertullian.

Montanism was denounced as a heresy by a Synod held in 230, and its followers were virtually excommunicated. However it continued strongly for some 200 years, but then began a decline that left it without a trace by the end of the 5th century. I wonder if the same fate may overtake the similar Pentecostal movement of our own time?

THE NOVATIANS

Novatian was a 3rd-century bishop, who composed the first full-length treatment of the doctrine of the Trinity. He was fully orthodox in belief, but argued strongly against welcoming back into the church the people who had apostasised during the Decian persecution (c. 250). He formed a breakaway group of churches that grew steadily and continued for some 300 years, until they were finally brought back into the orthodox fold. The 5th-century historian Socrates claims that Novatian himself endured cruel torments and suffered martyrdom under the persecution unleashed by the emperor Valerian.

THE ARIANS

Arius was a 4th century priest and teacher who argued that Christ was not eternal; rather, he was "begotten" by the Father, and therefore had a beginning. That is, there was a time when Jesus was not; therefore he must be less than God. His doctrines were sternly resisted, notably by the brilliant Athanasius; nonetheless, there were periods when Arians outnumbered orthodox Christians, and the bitter controversy did enormous harm to the church. The orthodox Trinitarian doctrine finally prevailed; but throughout church history various groups have espoused some form of Arianism - in our time, most notably the Jehovah's Witnesses.

THE DONATISTS

Donatus was a 4th-century African bishop who quarrelled with the official church leaders and formed a separatist church. He and his successors were so successful that for a century or more they were numerically dominant in North Africa. Despite vigorous persecution by the Catholic church they survived until they were destroyed by the Muslim conquests 400 years later. Donatus himself was banished from his see by the emperor Constantine (at the behest of the Catholic bishops), and died in exile.

THE NESTORIANS

Nestorianism sprang from the teachings of the 5th century patriarch of Constantinople, Nestorius. Because his doctrine of Christ differed from the views of the majority he was deposed from his see, and banished to Egypt, where he died in exile. But his ideas continued to find support, and his followers regrouped themselves in Persia, where they were beyond the reach of the Roman emperor and his bishops. The movement continued to flourish, and spread into Turkey, Arabia, and India. It was nearly obliterated by the Mongol invasions of the 13th and 14th centuries, but a remnant survived and continues to this day.

The Monophysites

The word means "one nature", and it describes a 5th century doctrine which held that Christ has only a divine nature, that he did not carry a human nature into heaven. The effect is to reduce his humanity to a mere garb, a kind of temporary costume that he assumed for a time, and then discarded. It solved some problems in the mystery of Christ's nature, but created many others, not least among them its contradiction of some clear statements in scripture. Nonetheless, for a time it gained wide popularity, and it is still held by some eastern European and Asian churches. Some of those groups, as you can see, endured for centuries before they finally either vanished, or were absorbed back into the mainstream.[84]

A WARNING TO THE MODERN CHURCH

Modern Pentecostals would do well to ponder this aspect of church history: the disappearance of once-flourishing movements, which in their time numbered millions of adherents and (in some cases) represented the greater number of Christians. There is no guarantee that today's Pentecostalism will survive to become the dominant part of the church. Indeed, historically, the opposite is more likely, that they will eventually fade away and be absorbed back into mainstream Christendom. Only diligent faithfulness to the call and purpose of God can hope to reverse that almost irresistible trend.

The same can be said of the greater part of the Protestant churches. After less than 500 years since the great Reformation of the 16th and 17th centuries, they have lost most of their momentum, and are struggling for survival. Five hundred years from now (if Jesus tarries), one wonders how much of the present cluster of denominations will still be bearing witness for Christ. Church

---

[84] For an illuminating study on the history of independent Christian churches, and various fringe groups across the centuries (who may well have been often recognised as the true church by God), see Churches Aglow Down the Ages, by Charles Taylor; pub. by the author; 1991.

history suggests that few of them will still be in existence. Most of them, like other great movements that flourished for a few centuries and then vanished without a trace, will be only an historical memory.

Even within the Catholic church during the first half-millennium the claims of the pope (the bishop of Rome) were disputed by the bishops (or popes) of Alexandria, Antioch, Constantinople, and Jerusalem.[85] Indeed, the Council of Nicea in 325 gave those five bishops equal primacy over the church, with each patriarch having the same level of authority.

THE RISE OF THE PAPACY

But the Roman popes began to assert a greater dominion. They started by claiming to be "first among equals", but then continued to escalate their claims until they were insisting upon true supremacy. However, that takes us into the next era of church history. Prior to the year 500 the bishop of Rome was not able to exert control over the other four bishops,[86] and a great struggle began to develop between the eastern and western segments of the church[87]

ITINERANT VOICES

A further factor complicating the structure of the early church, was the presence of various itinerant ministries, such as prophets, evangelists, teachers, and some claiming to be apostles. Several

---

[85] These men were called, with the bishop of Rome, the five Patriarchs of the church.

[86] Nor was he ever able to do so.

[87] The Roman Empire had by this time broken into two parts. There was the western empire, with its capital still at Rome, in which the Latin language and culture again became dominant. There was the eastern empire, with its capital at Constantinople, in which the Greek language and culture remained dominant.

references in the NT show that even while the apostles were still alive the churches often had trouble distinguishing between true and false ministries.[88] These itinerant preachers and prophets continued to be a problem, and various rules were devised in an effort to protect the churches from harm.[89] Paul appears to set apostles, prophets, and teachers at the head of the church (1 Co 12:28); but that ideal hardly survived the death of the last apostle. As I have already mentioned, early in the second century the process began of supplanting that charismatic leadership with the Episcopal authority of the bishops.

THE LOCAL CHURCH

IT'S MEMBERSHIP

Generally speaking, during the first 300 years, the church was free of class distinctions; membership and office were open to all who confessed faith in Christ. So it is not surprising to find a slave girl and her mistress standing hand in hand as they both face martyrdom for Christ.[90]

The full story of the two brave women (who were members of the Montanist group) is too long to tell on this page (it occupies several chapters), but here is a summary of it -

---

[88] Ac 20:29,30; Ro 16:17,18; 1 Co 11:18,19; 2 Co 11:3,4,13-14; 1 Jn 4:1-3,5; etc.

[89] Note again the passage I quoted in Chapter Two from the Didache Sec. 11,12,13.

[90] See "The Martyrdom of Perpetua and Felicitas," Ante-Nicene Fathers, Vol 3, pg 697ff, 705; and see also Nicene & Post-Nicene Fathers, Second Series, vol 1, pg 213ff. The story is also told in Foxe's Book of Martyrs, "Account of the Fifth General Persecution."

PERPETUA AND FELICITY

"Perpetua and Felicity (died 203) were martyrs of Carthage. Perpetua was a young married woman of twenty-two who had given birth to a son a few months before being arrested ... With Perpetua were a pregnant slave, Felicity, (and some men) ... After their arrest the Christians ... were imprisoned. Perpetua with her baby, concerned at her family's anxiety for her, said: `My prison became my palace to me and I would rather have been there than anywhere else.' ... Meanwhile Felicity gave birth to a girl in prison and the confessors enjoyed a last agape together. On the day of the Games they left the prison for the amphitheatre `joyfully as though they were on their way to heaven.' ... Animals were prepared for killing the prisoners: leopards and bears for the men, a mad heifer for the women. ... The heifer tossed Perpetua, but she got up and raised Felicity to her feet. Perpetua had been so absorbed in ecstasy that she seems to have been unaware of what had happened, for on her return to the gate of the amphitheatre she said: `When are we going to be thrown to that heifer, or whatever it is?' She refused to believe she had already suffered until she was shown the marks on her dress and on her body. ... (The mob demanded that the martyrs be killed. The young gladiator whose task it was to kill Perpetua could not do so because his hand was trembling too much. Perpetua herself placed the wavering knife at her throat and helped the young man to take her life.) `It was as though so great a

> woman ... could not be dispatched unless she herself were willing.'"[91]

But the lovely and joyful equality displayed by mistress and slave girl supporting each other in the terrible arena did not long survive. The rapidly growing wealth and power of Christianity after Constantine popularised it soon fractured the church into a hierarchy of pomp. The diocesan bishops became ever more haughty and elevated above their clergy, and the clergy too deemed themselves higher than their parishioners.

Following the example of the priesthood, the laity also insisted upon divisions of rank and wealth. A vivid example of this is seen in the use of the "holy kiss" - or as it came to be called, "the kiss of peace". In the following description of an early church service by Justin Martyr (c. 150), the equal fellowship and mutual respect among the people is plainly seen, and marked especially by the manner in which they all shared "a kiss" -

THE HOLY KISS - THE KISS OF PEACE

> "On the day which is called the day of the sun there is an assembly of all who live in the towns or in the country; and the memoirs of the apostles or the writings of the prophets are read, for as long as time permits. Then the reader ceases, and the president speaks, admonishing us and exhorting us to imitate these excellent examples. Then we arise all together and offer prayers ... both for ourselves and for ... all men everywhere, with all our hearts ... (Then) we salute each other with a kiss when we have ended the prayers ... We hold our common assembly on the day of the sun, because it is the same day (on

---

[91] The Oxford Dictionary of Saints, ed. David Hugh Farmer; Oxford University Press, Oxford, 1987; "Perpetua and Felicitas;" pg. 343, 344.

which) Jesus Christ our Saviour rose from the dead."[92]

By the beginning of the fourth century, men and women were obliged to sit in different parts of the church, and only those of the same sex were permitted to share the kiss. The clergy were forbidden to kiss the laity altogether, and were allowed only to greet the bishop -

THE APOSTOLIC CONSTITUTIONS (C. 325)

(a) " ... and after (the prayer) let the deacon say, 'Let us attend.' And let the bishop salute the church, and say, 'The peace of God be with you all.' And let the people answer, 'And with thy spirit.' Then let the deacons say to all, 'Salute ye one another with the holy kiss.' Then let the clergy salute (kiss) the bishop, the men of the laity salute the men, the women the women. And let the children stand at the reading-desk, and let another deacon stand by them, that they may not be disorderly."

ST AUGUSTINE

(b) Likewise, Augustine (c. 400) wrote -

"(The ungodly) resent the streams of people who gather in the church in a modest assembly, where there is a decent separation of the sexes, where they can hear how to live a good life on earth for a space, so that they may deserve hereafter to live a life of bliss for ever, and where the words of holy scripture

---

[92] Apology, Bk I, ch 65-67. This quotation, and those following, are all taken from The Anti-Nicene Fathers, Vol. 1-10; and from The Nicene and Post-Nicene Fathers, First & Second Series, 28 Volumes; all 1979 reprints by Eerdmans Pub. Co, Grand Rapids.

and of the teaching of righteousness are read aloud from a raised platform in the sight of all."[93]

THE SYNOD OF LAODICIEA

(c) The Synod of Laodicea (c. 375), established a formal liturgy for the churches, which included the following –

" ... there should then be offered the three prayers for the faithful, the first to be said entirely in silence, the second and third aloud, and then the kiss of peace is to be given. And after the presbyters have given the kiss of peace to the bishop, then the laity are to give it to one another ... "[94]

JEROME

Well before the 10th century, the kiss was restricted to the clergy; a tendency that is already apparent in a letter of Jerome to Theophilus, bishop of Alexandria -

"Does any turn his face away when you hold out your hand? Does any at the holy banquet offer you the kiss of Judas? At your approach the monks ... race to meet you ... You offer them a kiss; therefore they bow the neck."[95]

So formalities, rank, privilege, soon swamped the joyous liberty and mutual honour that characterised the first Christians.

---

93   City of God, Bk II, ch 28.

94   Canon 19. The laity at this time were separated, men on one side of the church and women on the other; thus the Canon presumes that the kiss of peace will be given only to a person of the same sex.

95   Letter LXXXII, written 399 A.D. Jerome is commending the bishop's gracious and loving rule over his monks.

IT'S SOCIAL WORK

There are many references in the Fathers, and in the writings of the enemies of the church, which tell of the extraordinary effort the early church put into caring for the poor, widows, orphans, prisoners, and so on. For this charity the Christians were revered by the more thoughtful and noble citizens, but equally reviled by their more numerous opponents. The general attitude of the ancient pagan world toward charitable works is shown in the following -

> "(The ungodly say) `Away with the poor and honest man! Tread him under foot! We will show no kindness to the widow, nor offer any respect to the grey hairs of old age. Victory belongs to the strong! Those who are weak are worthless. So let us make a snare for the good man. He keeps getting in our way; he is always interfering with our plans; he denounces us for breaking the law; he accuses us of betraying our birthright.[96] He claims to know God, and calls himself "the servant of the Lord". So he stands there, trying by his very presence to make us feel guilty. Just the sight of him is enough to make us feel sick. He chooses not to live the way other people do; he stands apart in all his ways. He treats us as if we were no better than counterfeit money; he avoids us as if we were lepers. He reckons that the righteous die happy, and boasts that he is a child of God. So let us put him to the test. Let us watch the outcome of his trial. If the good man really does belong to God, then let God reach out and deliver him from the power of his enemies. We will

---

96 Note that he is describing here godless Jews; it can be imagined what conditions were like outside Jewry, if such base attitudes could be found within it!

> subject him to insult and torture, then he will have a chance to display how much gentleness and patience he really has! He claims to have a Protector. We will give him an opportunity to prove it: we will condemn him to a foul death!'"[97]

That passage remained an accurate description, not only of backslidden Jews, but of most pagans, well into the Christian era. Far from admiring the gentleness and kindness of the Christians, they despised the church. Yet the Christians persisted with their charity, and slowly public opinion began to change. What had formerly been the cause of derision irresistibly became the cause of admiration. The church was now praised for works that once had brought it scorn.

---

97 Wisdom 2:10-20 (a Jewish "wisdom" writing, composed around the time of Christ).

Chapter Six:
SINGING SAINTS

TRAJAN AND PLINY

Early in the second century (c. 112) a persecution broke out against the Christians in Bithynia. The learned lawyer and governor Pliny was sent by the emperor Trajan to investigate the troubles. He examined several Christians, and was perplexed both by the lack of evidence of any real crime, and by the large number of people under trial. So he wrote to the emperor for advice -

"It is my custom, my lord emperor, to refer to you every question about which I find myself in doubt. ... This is the course I have adopted in the case of those brought before me as Christians ... if they persist, I sentence them to death. I am certain that, whatever it is they are admitting to, such perverse and stubborn obstinacy deserves to be punished. ... As for those who insisted that they neither were nor ever had been Christians, I thought it right to let them go. But first I made them repeat a prayer to the gods at my dictation ... and in particular to curse Christ; for those are things which (so it is said) people who are really Christians cannot be made to do. ... (The Christians) declared, however, that the sum of their supposed fault or error was no more than this: it was their habit on a certain day to assemble before daylight, then to recite a hymn[98] to Christ as a god; and to bind themselves by an oath - not for the commission of any crime, but to avoid theft, robbery, adultery, and never to break their word ... After this ceremony was

---

[98] The grammatical construction used by Pliny in the original document suggests some kind of regular pattern of words; perhaps a primitive liturgy of recitation and song.

concluded, they would then go to another place to share a meal together ... " [99]

Notice Pliny's description of the simple worship practices of the Christians. In his 4th century "Ecclesiastical History" Eusebius describes the same event, quoting the words of the African apologist Tertullian (early 3rd century) -

"Plinius Secundus, who was governor of the province, having condemned certain Christians, and deprived them of their dignity, was confounded by their great number, and in doubt what course he should pursue. He communicated the fact to Trajan the emperor, saying, that with the exception they were not willing to sacrifice (to the Roman gods), he found nothing criminal in them. He stated also this, that the Christians arose with the sun, and sang to Christ as to a god; and that for the purpose of keeping their discipline, they prohibited adultery, murder, overreaching, fraud, and all crimes like them. To this, Trajan wrote in reply, that the Christians should not be enquired after, but when they presented themselves they should be punished." [100]

Pliny, Tertullian, Eusebius, all confirm the simplicity of the worship of the early post-apostolic church: the Christians rose early in the morning and sang a hymn to Christ. Indeed, many aspects of the worship of the first Christians would seem strange to us -

THE FIRST CHURCH BUILDING

EXOTIC WORSHIP

I have already mentioned that the first known church building dates from around the year 230. It was a modified house, built in the Roman city of Dura-Europus, on the banks of the Euphrates.

---

[99] Adapted from various sources.
[100] Book III.33. Reprint of the 1850 edition by Baker Book House, Grand Rapids, 1977; pg. 119, 120.

Some walls were knocked out, and other changes made, to create a small sanctuary able to accommodate a congregation of about 65 people. Prior to this, almost all congregations met in houses. Few were large enough to require a rented hall. It is sobering to reflect on the fact that for 200 years the Christian assemblies were mostly house churches, probably numbering less than 50 people. From the middle of the 3rd century onward there is increasing record of the use of dedicated church buildings. But not until the time of Constantine was there any rapid expansion in designing and erecting churches.

Here are some other practices of the first Christians -

DISCIPLINE

They looked upon sin very seriously, seeing it not only as a crime against God, but also as a blow against the church. Public confession of fault was often required, accompanied by strict prayer and fasting. If the sin was serious enough, a period of penitence was imposed upon the sorrowing person, during which he or she was excluded from sharing in the Lord's Supper. In practice, this meant that when the time came for the Eucharist to be celebrated the defaulting Christian would be obliged to leave the meeting.

Even after the period of discipline had come to an end, the transgressor would still not be re-admitted to the communion table unless he or she gave full evidence of a change of heart and life.

A similar banishing from the eucharist was imposed upon people who were not yet baptised, or were still being catechised. After the bread and wine were consecrated in the communion service, portions of them were frequently taken out to members of the congregation who were ill, or in prison for their faith, or who for some other reason were unable to be present. And in remembrance of the six weeks that Jesus spent fasting and praying in the wilderness, many churches adopted the custom of fasting for 40 days before Good Friday.

A common practice was to gather the congregation at the burial place of a deceased member on the anniversary of his or her death, and there hold a worship service. Hymns were sung, scriptures read, prayers offered, a meal eaten, perhaps a short homily delivered, and alms were collected and taken out to the poor as a memorial of the departed saint.

Such practices of course, presuppose small congregations who could gather in full around a single grave.

HYMNS

The few copies that we have of ancient hymns suggest that the serious temper of the times swayed the church toward serious songs. Perhaps the oldest one extant (apart from a few lines in the New Testament) is the following, composed by the priest Clement of Alexandria (c. 200), who was also one of the most influential teachers of the early 3rd century -

> Bridle of colts untamed,
>
> Over our wills presiding;
>
> Wing of unwandering birds,
>
> Our flight securely guiding.
>
> Rudder of youth unbending,
>
> Firm against adverse shock;
>
> Shepherd, with wisdom tending
>
> Lambs of thy royal flock:
>
> Thy simple children bring
>
> In one, that they may sing
>
> In solemn lays
>
> Their hymns of praise

With guileless lips to Christ their King.[101]

STRUCTURE

The *Didache* shows that early in the second century, while worship was still simple and plain, there was already an accepted use of formal structures and of standard prayers and responses -

THE "DIDACHE" ON THE EUCHARIST

> "Concerning the eucharist, give thanks in this way. First for the cup: We give thanks to you Father for the sacred vine of your servant David, which you have presented to us through your servant Jesus. (Then the congregation will say:) Unto you be all glory for ever!"[102]

The same liturgy forbade anyone who was not baptised to share in the cup and bread at the eucharist. It put the same prohibition upon anyone who had an ongoing dispute with a Christian brother or sister.

JUSTIN MARTYR AND AN EARLY CHURCH SERVICE

Justin Martyr (in the passage I have already partly cited), included the following elements in his description of the early second century church at worship:

> ➢ the church met on Sunday, in celebration of the resurrection of Christ on the first day of the week

---

[101] Clement himself calls his poem a hymn, to be offered to the Lord in thanksgiving for his guidance and instruction. It is appended to his work, "The Instructor", and is its climax, save for a final poem, which is a prayer to Christ, the Instructor. The lines quoted above are about one quarter of the full length of the hymn. From the Ante-Nicene Fathers, Vol. II, pg. 295.

[102] The beginning of Section Nine, which continues on through another Section.

- the service began with a time of introductory prayer, followed by everyone greeting each other with a holy kiss
- thanksgiving was offered for the bread and wine of the eucharist, accompanied by a "long prayer" of dedication to Christ
- at the end of those prayers, the congregation gave assent by speaking a formal *Amen!*
- the wine was mingled with water, and then the deacons distributed the bread and the cup among the people; some was also carried off, and taken to those who were absent for some good reason
- no one was allowed to share in the eucharist who did not fully subscribe to the teachings of the church, or who had not been baptised
- an offering was taken from those who had much to share with those who had little
- there was an extended reading from the scriptures, which included "the memoirs of the apostles, and the writings of the prophets"
- the leader of the congregation preached from the scriptures, exhorting the people and admonishing them to righteousness
- the sermon was followed by another time of vigorous prayer and thanksgiving
- any surplus funds were kept on hand to help orphans, widows, the sick, Christians suffering imprisonment, and any who were in need.

CYPRIAN ON THE EUCHARIST

Cyprian, writing c. 255, insisted that nothing may be done in the eucharist except what conforms to the gospel, and that the wine must be mingled with water in memory of the cross. If either water or wine is missing, then he declared that the eucharist was not valid. He raised the issue, because some churches had taken to using only water in their dawn eucharists. They had a good reason for doing so: if the devout happened to meet some soldiers on the way home then no smell of wine on their breath would betray them as Christians. Other churches had taken to holding an evening eucharist instead, and to using wine there, since the pagans themselves all had wine with their evening meals.

Cyprian protested against both practices; first, because both wine and water were needed to provide a true memorial of Calvary; and second, because Jesus rose in the morning, not the evening.[103]

HIPPOLYTUS AND WATER BAPTISM IN ROME

BAPTISM

Hippolytus (c. 215), in his "Apostolic Traditions" (4-6,21-22,41), provides a graphic description of the way people had to prepare for baptism, and of how the ceremony was performed in Rome at that time:

> ➢ at least *three years* of catechism had to precede the ceremony;
>
> ➢ just before the event, the candidates had to undergo a time of fasting, followed by an all-night prayer vigil before the morning of their baptism;
>
> ➢ at dawn, a ritual of exorcism was performed, to take authority over all the works of Satan;
>
> ➢ after stepping into the baptistry each candidate had to undergo a long series of prayers, questions testing his or her faith, and various anointings with oil;

---

[103] Letter 63:2,13,15,16. For an extensive treatment of the eucharist, see also Cyril (c. 350), "Catechesis" 23:1-9,11,19-22.

- baptism was by immersion in cold running water if possible, otherwise in still water; if there was insufficient water, then by pouring or sprinkling (the baptistry in the oldest known church building is only deep enough to stand in, with the water calf-high, which suggests that it was poured over the candidate);
- sometimes the candidate was baptised two or three times in succession, in response to a series of affirmations of faith;
- during the ceremony the candidates, both men and women, were quite naked;[104]
- after being baptised, the candidate was again anointed with oil, and a new robe was given to him or her to mark the beginning of life as a new creation in Christ;
- straightway the candidates then proceeded to the church where they celebrated their first eucharist;
- all of this, in the half-light of the dawn, and accompanied by music and hymns, was done with a high level of excitement, keen anticipation, and joy.

By the end of the 5th century the simple and spontaneous worship of the first two centuries had become quite formal and liturgical, though still not as elaborate as it was to become in later centuries. There also remained many differences in the worship style and practices followed in different parts of the church.[105]

---

[104] Remember that in Rome at that time few homes had their own toilet or bathroom facilities. Most citizens had to use the public toilets and the public baths, where there was a free mingling of the sexes. So they were all well used to seeing naked members of the opposite sex.

105 See the Addendum to my book, The Worship Leader, which contains a number of passages from the Fathers, plus many references.

ASCETICISM

One unfortunate development in the early church was a growing asceticism, which heavily influenced the entire church from about the middle of the second century onward to the time of Constantine. When the emperor removed all legal sanctions from the church, ascetic practices lost their popularity. They became more and more confined to the monasteries, which were set up primarily for the purpose of allowing their inhabitants to separate themselves from the world. The result was disastrous. A kind of double standard was established: *first*, the special holiness that the men and women in the monasteries were thought to possess; and *second*, the inferior, rather sin-smirched and guilt-stricken holiness that everyone else had to be content with.[106]

NOTABLE ASCETICS

One hermit, hoping to subdue the flesh and achieve a state of holiness, spent 10 years in a bucket slung between two poles.[107] James and Alexander of Cyr imposed upon themselves the sentence of *standing* in the open for the rest of their lives.[108] Acepsemus shut himself in a cell for 60 years, refusing to see or speak to anyone[109] while another hermit lived alone in a cave on the top of a mountain, and never once turned his face toward the west. They all became a pattern for many others who locked themselves alone in caves for life, slept on beds of thorns, laced their food with bitter herbs, twisted thorns and thistles into their garments, and inflicted on themselves countless other pains.

---

106 For teaching on ascetic austerity, see Origen, Tertullian in the "Ante-Nicene Fathers"; Clement of Alexandria (ibid, vol 2, pg 237 ff); and for other examples see the stories of Hilarion ("Post-Nicene Fathers", vol 6, pg 303); and Anthony (Latourette, vol 1, pg 225-226).

107 Theodoret, "Philotheus" 28.

108 Ibid. "Ecc. Hist." 17-21. Astonishingly, these and other ascetics apparently succeeded in keeping their vows.

109 Ibid. 4.28.

One of the most renowned hermits was St Simeon Stylites (390-459), who sat on a 60-foot pillar for 36 years. I will return to him below; but in the meantime note that he was outdone by St Simeon the Younger. The early historian Evagrius says that while Simeon was still a child he befriended and tamed a young panther, which he led to a nearby monastery. The preceptor, who was ensconced on a column himself at the time, saw in this a sign of special sanctity. He invited the boy to join him on his column, which Simeon agreed to do, and then spent the next 68 years on pillars of ever-increasing height, including 45 years on his last. Many miracles of healing, exorcisms, accurate prophecies, and the like were attributed to him.

But both Simeons were exceeded by St Alipius, who combined the idea of *standing* in the open with that of a *pillar*, and so he stood on his pillar for 53 years, until he lost the use of both his feet, after which he spent his last 14 years lying only on one side of his body.

GOD'S ATHLETES

Evagrius writes further -

> "(There are some) who individually seclude themselves in chambers of so limited a height and width that they can neither stand upright nor lie down at ease, confining their existence to 'dens and caves of the earth', as says the apostle. Some too take up their dwelling with the wild beasts ... Another mode has also been devised, one which reaches to the utmost extent of resolution and endurance; for transporting themselves to a scorched wilderness, and covering only those parts which nature requires to be concealed, both men and women leave the rest of their persons exposed both to excessive frosts and scorching blasts, regardless alike of heat and cold.
>
> "They, moreover, cast off the ordinary food of mankind, and feed upon the produce of the ground,

> whence they are termed *Grazers*, allowing themselves no more than is barely sufficient to sustain life. ... I will mention still another class ... persons who, when by virtue they have attained to a condition exempt from passion, return to the world.... They (then) frequent the public baths, mostly mingling and bathing with women, since they have attained to such an ascendancy over their passions as to possess dominion over nature, and neither by sight, touch, or even embracing of the female, to relapse into their natural condition. It (is) their desire to be men and among men and women among women, and to participate in both sexes. In short, by a life thus all excellent and divine, virtue exercises a sovereignty in opposition to nature ..."[110]

The heroic if misguided exploits of these incredible men and women led to them being often called *"athletes of God"*, for indeed their self-denial and personal discipline surpassed that of the fiercest competitors in the games.

CYPRIAN DE MULVERTON

> "Cyprian de Mulverton, fifth prior of the monastery of Saint Francis, a prelate of singular sanctity ... vowed never again to behold with earthly eyes the blessed light of heaven, nor to dwell longer with his fellow men. ... He kept his vow. Out of the living rock that sustained the saintly structure, beneath the chapel of the monastery, was another chapel wrought, and thither, after bidding an eternal farewell to the world ... the holy man retired.

---

[110] "Ecclesiastical History"; Bohn's Ecclesiastical Library; London, 1854; pg 285, 286.

" ... Ascetic to the severest point to which nature's endurance could be stretched, Cyprian even denied himself repose. He sought not sleep, and knew it only when it stole on him unawares. His couch was the flinty rock; and long afterwards, when the zealous resorted to the sainted prior's cell, and were shown those sharp and jagged stones, they marvelled how one like unto themselves could rest, or even recline upon their points without anguish. ... His limbs were clothed in a garb of horsehair of the coarsest fabric; his drink was the dank drops that oozed out of the porous walls of his cell; and his sustenance, such morsels as were bestowed upon him by the poor. ... No fire was suffered, where perpetual winter reigned. None were admitted to his nightly vigils; none witnessed any act of penance; nor were any groans heard to issue from that dreary cave; but the knotted blood-stained thong, discovered near his couch, too plainly betrayed in what manner those long nights were spent."[111]

Likewise, in the 6th century, in convents, it was not uncommon for a nun to have herself bricked into a small space, leaving only a tiny slit through which food was passed, and there remain until death. Possession of such a "living relic" brought enormous prestige to a convent, along with large numbers of pilgrims, and of course much additional revenue.

ST SIMEON STYLITES

But let us sum it all up by returning to the best known of the hermits, St Simeon Stylites -

---

[111] I have lost the source of this quote, except that I think it comes from one of W. H. Ainsworth's novels.

The son of a shepherd, while he was still a teenager tending sheep Simeon had a vision in which he was called to devote his life to the service of God. He responded by joining a monastery as a servant, where he remained for two years. Becoming discontent with its laxity of rule, he moved to a more austere hermitage. There he practised harsher mortifications than any of the other monks, until he nearly died from twisting a rope of palm leaves so tightly around his waist that it sank beneath his flesh. It took the monks three days to remove the rope by softening his skin with liquids, and then by cutting out the leaves with a knife. When his health recovered, the abbot expelled him.

Simeon next spent three years chained to a rock on top of a mountain; but throngs of pilgrims, climbing to his retreat and begging him to pray for them, kept on disturbing his solitude. So he called for a blacksmith to release him from his chain, found a stone column about three metres high, built a small railed platform on top of it, mounted it, and made it his home. There he remained for 4 years, dependent entirely upon disciples for the meagre sustenance that was conveyed to him by a ladder.

Finding himself still too accessible he built a second pillar, 6 metres high, where he spent 3 years; then a third (10 metres high), where he spent 10 years; and a fourth (18 metres), where he spent his last 20 years.

During lent he fasted absolutely, spending the first two weeks standing upright praising God; the next two sitting; and last two (owing to growing weakness from the fast) lying horizontal. Every day throughout the year he repeatedly bowed his body in prayer, while wearing a heavy iron collar. He was known to prostrate himself more than 1000 times in succession. Unwashed, except by rain and dew, exposed to all the elements, clothed in rags, unshorn, he crawled with vermin.

Twice each day he preached to the multitudes who thronged at the foot of his pillar, including emperors and princes. He healed so many sick people that a mountain of crutches, sticks, and supports were piled at the foot of his pillar. Under his preaching thousands were converted to Christ. Influential letters poured from his pen, arguing vigorously for orthodox theology, rebuking corrupt rulers, demanding righteous policies. His preaching (perhaps surprisingly) was practical and compassionate and his doctrine was sound. He died, still on his pillar, while bowing before God in prayer.[112]

THE FAILURE OF ASCETICISM

How sobering that is! Can such a man die? Yes, he can, and he must, as all men, great and small, sinner or saint, must die; and he now shares the common home of all, the grave -

>What is the gain of our coming and going?
>
>Where is the weft of our life's warp?
>
>In the circle of the spheres the lives of so many good men
>
>Burn and become dust, but where is the smoke?

>There was a water-drop, it joined the sea,
>
>A speck of dust, it was fused with the earth;
>
>What of your entering and leaving this world?
>
>A fly appeared, and disappeared.[113]

In the end the ascetic experiment failed, although its ancient fibres are still threaded through modern church life, strangling the spiritual vitality of the saints. St Simeon, and all the ascetics, made the bitter discovery that none of their privations had

---

[112] Perhaps the best portrayal of the inner feelings and motives of the hermits can be found in Lord Tennyson's deeply moving and sensitive poem, St Simeon Stylites.

[113] The Ruba'iyat of Omar Khayyam; tr. Peter Avery & John Heath-Stubbs; Penguin Classics, 1983; quatrains 18 & 41

advanced them even one comma in righteousness. Emperor or slave, hermit or politician, wealthy or starving, scholar or peasant - the same word is true of all: if righteousness is to belong to any of us it must come by the free grace of God. We are either made righteous by his gift to us in Christ, or we must for ever remain unrighteous.

Chapter Seven:
CHURCH CONTROVERSIES

In the year 1553 the Spanish-born theologian and physician, Servetus, was arrested by order of John Calvin (the great Reformer), tried for heresy, condemned, and put to death at the stake outside the walls of Geneva. Ironically, Servetus had fled to Geneva to escape the Roman Catholic Inquisition, which was also eager to burn him to ashes. Both camps denounced him for holding doctrines that (in their view) made him unfit to live! He deeply loved Christ, and as the flames surged around him he cried, "O Jesus, thou Son of the Eternal God, have compassion for me!" Before his death, while still on trial, he said to his judges, "I will burn, but this is a mere incident. We shall continue our discussions in eternity!" [114]

Indeed, some of the controversies that have torn the church over the years probably cannot be resolved this side of the resurrection, including some of those we look at in this chapter. One of the issues that is as heatedly debated today as ever it was in the past is the question of

---

[114] Calvin, to his credit, did plead for a less cruel method of execution for the "heretic". But Servetus' death was not in vain. It provoked a storm of protest, and caused many thoughtful people to begin calling for much greater tolerance of doctrinal diversity among Christians. Servetus after all, though he called into question the doctrine of the Trinity, and some other established concepts, nonetheless declared himself a deeply committed Christian.

CONTROVERSIAL ISSUES

THE CHARISMATA

The charismata [115] have never wholly vanished from the church, for references to their existence can be found in every century; but it is nonetheless clear that a movement away from overt and public charismatic manifestations had begun early in the second century. One notable exception has been mentioned already: the Montanist movement, which began with the self-declared prophet Montanus, about the middle of the second century. He announced a new outpouring of the Holy Spirit, and a restoration of all the gifts of the Spirit. Glossolalia and prophecies were experienced, and many miracles of healing were claimed. Montanus also insisted that his followers should separate themselves as much as possible from the world, in the belief that the second advent would soon occur. He gave prominence to women in his churches, and may even have had female bishops. The growth of Montanism was initially slow, because of its stern austerity, its demand for constant fastings, its suspicion of marriage, and its "otherworldliness". But then a fierce persecution struck the whole church, which many interpreted as a sign of the end of the world, and people began to flock into the Montanist churches.

As the movement grew in popularity, opposition also grew, until in 230 Montanists were virtually excommunicated; but the sect nonetheless continued to flourish for more than a century, and its history continued for a further two centuries, before it finally vanished, absorbed back into the mainstream. But in the meantime, Montanism had a lasting impact upon the church, in several ways -

---

[115] The "charismata" are the cluster of supernatural gifts that the Holy Spirit expressed through the church during the days of the apostles, and which "pentecostals" and "charismatics" claim are still available to the church today. - see 1 Co 12:4-11; etc.

(1) The excesses of the movement, and its sometimes dubious doctrine and practice alarmed the majority church and created an acceleration of the anti-charismatic process.

(2) Largely in response to Montanism (especially during the time of its greatest expansion in the early third century), the majority church became "catholic". It drew itself together more tightly under the steadying control of the bishops, and rejected the disturbing influence of prophets. In opposition to the Montanist emphasis on withdrawal from secular society, and their focus on the end of the world, the Catholic churches searched for ways to come to terms with the world, and to live within it.

(3) The reaction against Montanism caused an increase of the bishop's authority and a corresponding reduction in the role of inspired prophets, which in turn hastened the move toward a fixed canon of scripture, and a rejection of the idea of ongoing revelation.

(4) Montanists produced the first major theologies of the Holy Spirit, and strongly influenced the development of Trinitarian doctrine; but they also made officialdom suspicious of expectations of Christ's immediate return; and the anti-charismatic prejudice it caused has continued to the present time.

THE CANON

At first there was no felt need for a fixed canon, for the church generally accepted the Jewish scriptures, which then included several books that are no longer accepted into the Hebrew Bible (they are known generally as the Old Testament Apocrypha). Various Christian writings were steadily added to the Jewish books, including the gospels, several apostolic letters, apocalypses, and so on.

For a long time, different churches actually had different collections of sacred writings. However, two factors developed that compelled the churches to settle upon an agreed corpus of scripture, against which all its beliefs and practices could be tested:

HERESIES

The increasing number of sects, cults, and strange doctrines, put pressure upon the churches to accept only those writings that contained undeniable evidence of being divinely inspired.

PERSECUTIONS

No one wanted to die for a spurious document, so great pains were exerted to authenticate and endorse only those writings that could be proved to have been written by an apostle, or had some kind of apostolic endorsement, or for some other reason were deemed worthy of inclusion in the canon. For a long time, for example, the authenticity of the gospel of John was doubted, along with that of the Apocalypse, Hebrews, James, 2 Peter, and 2 & 3 John. By contrast, other books from both Jewish and Christian writings that are now rejected, were accepted in many early churches - for example, The Wisdom of Sirach and the Shepherd of Hermas.

Finally, the general decision of the churches was:

> - to accept into the OT only those books that the Jews themselves admitted into their canon; and
> - to fix the NT canon at the 27 books it currently contains

The first complete list of those 27 NT books is dated 367 (although full agreement on the list was actually not reached until some time after that date). The list is found in a letter that Athanasius, bishop of Alexandria, wrote to his people at Easter of that year (it is the 39th in a series of Easter circulars) -

> " ... (after listing the OT books, he continues) ... Again it is not tedious to speak of the books of the New Testament. These are ... (then follows the list of 27) ... These are the fountains of salvation, that they who thirst may be satisfied with the living words they contain. In these alone is proclaimed the doctrine of godliness. Let no man add to these, neither let him take ought from these ... (There) are other books besides these not indeed included in the

Canon, but appointed by the Fathers to be read by those who newly join us, and who wish for instruction in the word of godliness. The Wisdom of Solomon, and the Wisdom of Sirach, and Esther and Judith and Tobit, and that which is called the Teaching of the Apostles, and the Shepherd. But the former, my brethren, are included in the Canon, the latter being merely read ... "[116]

DOCTRINES

The first 300 years were years of controversy. Almost every doctrine held by the church was debated and contested. Endless heresies sprang up, flourished, vanished, only to appear again, and again. Some of the issues argued about were -

ESCHATOLOGY

For 300 years the hope of Christ's near return was kept alive in the church; his coming was expected any day, every day. But three factors worked to change this expectation:

- ➢ a reaction against the extreme views that were preached with much passion but sometimes little sense by such groups as the Montanists;
- ➢ the constant recalculation of dates that proved fruitless;[117]
- ➢ and the cessation of the persecutions.

For most people, those developments caused the initial hope of a heavenly kingdom to change into a belief that the church itself would usher in an earthly paradise. After the 4th century, hope in

---

[116] Post-Nicene Fathers, vol 4, pg 552.

117 See my book "Oracles Galore", which traces unfulfilled predictions of Christ's return across the entire span of church history.

the nearness of Christ's return tended to wax and wane in parallel with changes in society.[118]

BAPTISM

Immersion was originally the universal practice, if possible in running water,[119] but sprinkling was allowed. Fairly early, infant baptism was also allowed (probably following the example of Jewish circumcision, and perhaps also influenced by the pressure of the persecutions), and this gradually became the dominant form.

In some parts of the church, and at some periods, there was also a strong tendency to postpone baptism until the closest possible moment before death. This was based upon a belief (which became surprisingly widespread) that post-baptismal sin could not be forgiven. For example, the emperor Constantine delayed baptism until just before his death, for which he has sometimes been accused of compromise; but Gibbon comes closer to the reason:

> " ... The delay in his baptism may be justified by the maxims and practice of ecclesiastical antiquity. The sacrament of baptism was supposed to contain a full and absolute expiation of sin; and the soul was instantly restored to its original purity, and entitled to the promise of eternal salvation. Among the proselytes of Christianity there were many who judged it imprudent to precipitate a salutary rite, which could not be repeated; to throw away an inestimable privilege, which could never be recovered ... "[120]

---

[118] Note: the church has held consistently to the doctrine of Christ's return; but the hope of an imminent fulfilment of the promise has fluctuated greatly.

[119] See the *Didache*, sec. 7.

[120] Quoted in Post-Nicene Fathers, vol 1, pg 556.

Eusebius has recorded Constantine's speeches, made prior to and after his baptism.[121]

THE EUCHARIST

At the end of the 5th century the nature of the eucharist was still unresolved; similar differences to those that still divide the modern church were apparent among the views of various teachers. There was also controversy over the number of the sacraments: some argued that there were but two (baptism and the eucharist); others contended for a larger number (up to as many as twelve). That controversy, too, has continued to the present time.

CHRIST

The main centre of doctrinal storm was Christ himself. The church recognised that Christ alone made Christianity unique. Other faiths, like the various "mystery" religions might share many things with Christianity, such as baptism, love feasts, a belief in immortality, a promise of heaven, and the like. But no other religion had anything or anyone comparable to Christ.

Yet that very uniqueness brought special difficulty to the task of trying to define just who Jesus is (cp. 1 Ti 3:16). Since there has never been any other like Jesus, there were no precedents to follow in the struggle to understand the mystery of his incarnation. Hence the church found itself constantly fighting three main heresies:

- ➢ the gospel stories were simply myths, like those of the familiar Greek legends;
- ➢ the humanity of Jesus was not real; he only appeared to be a man, but he was actually and altogether divine; or
- ➢ the reverse of the former, that the humanity of Jesus was total; he was only a man, and not in any sense God.

---

[121] Ibid. The Life of Constantine, bk 4, ch 62, 63

For most Christians the issue was finally resolved by the statement of the doctrine of the Trinity that was formulated at the great Council of Chalcedon (451). The Council affirmed both the full humanity and full deity of Christ, but did not attempt to define how such a mystery could be. The Council declared in part -

> "We all with one accord teach men to acknowledge one and the same Son, our Lord Jesus Christ, at once complete in Godhead and complete in manhood, truly God and truly man, consisting also of a reasonable soul and body; of one substance with the Father as regards his Godhead, and at the same time of one substance with us as regards his manhood; like us in all respects, apart from sin; as regards his Godhead, begotten of the Father before the ages, but yet as regards his manhood begotten, for us men and for our salvation, of Mary the Virgin... the characteristics of his two natures being preserved and coming together to form one person and subsistence, not as parted or separated into two persons, but one and the same Son and Only-begotten God the Word, Lord Jesus Christ ... "[122]

SUNDAY

Jewish Christians initially adhered to sabbath-worship. But by the middle of the second century Sunday had become for most Christians the chief day of worship. It was honoured as the day of the Lord's resurrection.

Thus we read:

> ➤ Justin Martyr (c. 150): "On the day called Sunday, all the people, whether they live in the city or the country, gather together in one place. There the memoirs of the apostles are read ... The day upon which we all meet in common

---

[122] From Bettenson, op. cit. pg. 51.

assembly is Sunday ... because that is the day upon which Jesus Christ our Saviour rose from the dead."[123]

- Tertullian (c. 200): "Since it is a well-known fact that we pray facing towards the east, and that we make Sunday a day of celebration, some people suppose that we Christians worship the sun."[124]

- The Didache (c. 100): "The apostles also gave us this rule: on the first day of the week let the people gather for the reading of the holy scriptures and for the eucharist."[125]

- Ignatius (c. 100): "If you are a friend of Christ, then set aside the Lord's day for sacred celebration, for it is the resurrection day, the queen and the sovereign over all the days of the week ... Those who grew up knowing only the traditional ways have now discovered a new hope, for they no longer keep the old Sabbath, but now they continually observe the Lord's day, the day on which our life sprang into existence with Christ ... "[126]

- Melito, bishop of Sardis (c. 170), wrote a treatise commending Sunday worship.

- Constantine enacted legislation requiring cessation of most forms of labour (except agricultural) on Sunday; he also endorsed Sunday as a proper day of worship, and it became more and more established as part of the law of the empire, until (probably) sometime in the 5th century its sanctity was finally fixed by law.

---

[123] Apology I.65-67.
[124] Ad Nationes, Bk. I.13.
[125] Section Two.
[126] Magnesians 9, combining the longer and the shorter versions.

MARY

By the end of the 5th century a cult of martyrs and of the Virgin Mary had developed. Prayers were being addressed to these persons and Mary was being called the "Mother of God". Strong dissent was raised against such practices by many thoughtful and prudent persons; but the cults were too popular to be demolished and remain firmly entrenched still in Roman Catholicism and among the Orthodox churches.

DUALISM

Under the influence of Greek philosophy (especially Neo-Platonism[127]) the church became heavily infiltrated by mysticism, and by a disjunction between matter and spirit. Thus a dualism was created between the mystics and the more prosaic members of the church, and between flesh and spirit - a dualism that is still rampant in our time.

LEGALISM

The original gospel of grace quickly became entangled in a doctrine of salvation by good works; legalism became endemic in the church, with only a few voices raised in protest.

CONCLUSION

Thus the 5th century came to an end. The church was triumphant everywhere. The imperial persecutions were vanquished. Heretics were crushed. The remaining pockets of paganism were being ruthlessly purged. The face of human society had been astonishingly changed, and would never be the same again.

---

[127] A school of philosophy that added a strong concept of monotheism, and of the transcendence of God, to the basic thought of Plato. It began before the Christian era, but began to reach its ascendancy in the 4th and 5th centuries.

One dramatic example of this change can be found in the eradication of the gladiatorial games, which is strikingly illustrated by the story of Telemachus -

THE STORY OF TELEMACHUS

> "In those dark and shameful days the great white Coliseum, rising storey after storey from the ground, with enormous galleries inside capable of holding 50,000 people, was a wondrous sight. Here came all Rome to see the great wild beasts set loose to tear one another to pieces. Here came the gladiators, strong men trained to fight until one of them was killed. Here the Christians were once thrown alive to the lions. No place in the world has seen more cruel sights than this. ... (On a certain day the cheerful crowds flocked to the great arena for a splendid display.) ... There was a great hunting of beasts and a wonderful performance, as in the olden time, when suddenly there came out of one of the narrow passages leading into the arena gladiators, with spears and swords. The joy of the people knew no bounds, and they shouted with delight.
>
> "Then there happened a strange thing. Into the middle of the arena came an old man, bare-headed and bare-footed, calling upon the people to prevent the shedding of blood. The crowd shrieked at him to stop his preaching and to go away. The gladiators came forward and forced him aside, but still the old man came between them. The gladiators struck him down; a storm of stones fell upon him and the old man perished before the eyes of Rome.
>
> "He was a hermit, named Telemachus, one of those holy men who, tired of the wickedness of the world, had gone to live in the hills. Coming to Rome to visit the sacred shrines, he had seen the people

flocking to the Coliseum, and, pitying them for their cruelty, had gone out to stop it or to die in the attempt.

"He died, but his work was done. All that was best in Rome was stirred by the sight of the hermit slain in the arena, and there was no more slaughter in the great circus. It was the last fight that was ever held in the Colosseum."[128]

So the world was changing, and the church was dominant. But it had also paid a high price. It began with the blood of the martyrs; but it continued with the far more tragic cost: the loss of its spiritual virginity. The eager, joyous, pure, simple, and courageous church of the first two centuries had now become a ponderous empire-wide organisation. Corruption was already eating at its structures, its doctrines, and its practices. Against this sad state many brave voices would be raised, but mostly in vain. Christendom was about to enter a thousand years of darkness, broken only by occasional flashes of light, out of which it would not emerge until the time of the Reformation.[129]

---

128 The only historical account of this event is in Theodoret, "Ecclesiastical History" Bk. V.26; Post-Nicene Fathers, Vol III. The story as told above, which takes some historical liberties, comes from Arthur Mee's "Children's Encyclopaedia", Vol. III; 1963 edition; pg. 207,208. The story is thought to be generally true, and if the brave death of Telemachus did not by itself stop the gladiatorial contests, it certainly was a strong catalyst toward that happy outcome. The incident happened during the reign of the emperor Honorius (393-423), who did issue the decree that banned the use of gladiators in the arena.

129 Latourette, op. cit. pg. 362.

PART TWO:

THE EXPANDING CHURCH (A.D. 500-1000)

Eternal Time, that wastest without waste,
That art, and art not! diest, and livest still;
Most slow of all; and yet of greatest haste;
Both ill and good; and neither good nor ill:
How can I justly praise thee, or dispraise?
Dark are thy nights, but bright and clear thy days.

Both free and scarce, thou giv'st and tak'st again;
Thy womb that all doth breed, is tomb to all;
What so by thee hath life, by thee is slain;
From thee do all things rise, by thee they fall!
Constant, inconstant, moving, standing still;
Was, Is, shall Be, do thee both breed and kill!

I lose thee, while I seek to find thee out;
The farther off, the more I follow thee;
The faster hold, the greater cause of doubt!
Was, Is, I know; but Shall I cannot see.
All things by thee are measured: thou, by none;
All are in thee! thou, in thyself alone![130]

---

[130] Composed in 1602, nothing is known about the author except his or her initials, which were A.W.

Chapter Eight:
MULTITUDES CONVERTED

WHY STUDY CHURCH HISTORY?

INTRODUCTION

Let me repeat the question asked at the beginning of these studies, and give a little different answer to it: why study church history? Because

- it shows how the church came to be what it is today;
- it demonstrates what is right and wrong in Christian conduct;
- it reveals strategies for world evangelism that are bad and shows those that are good;
- it is an inspiring and challenging story;
- it helps to remove bigotry, for it is, as Earl Cairne has said, "a liberalising study;"
- and perhaps best of all, it inspires great confidence in the eventual triumph of the church over all her foes.

Travel with me back to the start of the second half-millennium of Christian witness. How much has happened since the Day of Pentecost 450 years earlier! The church is now co-extensive with the Roman Empire, having already overcome many powerful foes, and it has begun to spread into ever more distant lands. Here is a summary picture of the scene around the year 500 -

THE SCENE IN THE YEAR 500

A dramatic change occurred in church affairs after Constantine the Great, the first Christian emperor[131], granted religious freedom to all his subjects in 313, and began to favour the church with various subsidies, a practice that was continued by his successors. After Constantine, the clergy were exempted from civil obligations, Sunday became a day of worship and rest, and in 380 Theodosius the Great made Christianity the official religion of the state.

By the year 500 the barbarian invasions that were to destroy the Western Roman Empire had begun; yet the church had already shown success in converting the savage invaders to Christ, and then in reversing the process by itself invading foreign lands with the gospel. For example:

ULFILAS

- Ulfilas, in the 4th century, is reputed to have won the entire tribe of the pagan Visigoths to Arian Christianity! He invented an alphabet for the language of the Goths, so that they could be given the scriptures in their own tongue.

- by at least the late 3rd century missionaries had reached the British Isles, and had converted many of the Celtic tribes to the gospel.

ST PATRICK

St Patrick (son of a British town-councillor and deacon, and grandson of a priest) first went to Ireland when he was a boy, as the prisoner of a band of raiders. He was sold into slavery, but after six years escaped and sailed to Gaul, where he studied for the priesthood. After his ordination he was sent

---

[131] This is usually accepted as true; however, there is some reason to suppose that the emperor Philip the Arabian (died 249) may have been a Christian. His brief reign of five years, following upon several years of severe persecution, was at least marked by friendship toward the church.

back to Ireland (circa 435) as a missionary and remained there for the rest of his life. His ministry was remarkably successful. On one occasion he used a shamrock (which has three leaves coming out of one stem) to illustrate the Trinity, and thus brought about the conversion of a powerful Irish chieftain. Since then, the shamrock has been the national emblem of Ireland. Many improbable legends gathered around his name, including his eviction of all snakes from Ireland by a staff that Christ gave him. One Easter, using the same staff, he supernaturally kindled a fire on a hill that was formerly sacred to pagans, which led many to repent and embrace the gospel.

ST COLUMBA

From Ireland, St Columba embarked in 565 to carry the gospel to Scotland. He was a charismatic figure, tall, handsome, powerfully built, strong in both scholarship and leadership. He built a great monastery on the island of Iona, off the coast of Scotland, and there, apart from occasional journeys abroad, he remained until his death. Many miracles of healing and exorcism were attributed to him, and he laboured indefatigably to spread the gospel, planting churches, and training missionaries. He wrote many books, hymns, poems, and prayers, including the following passionate lines -

"Almighty Father, Son, and Holy Ghost, eternal ever blessed gracious God; to me the least of saints, to me allow that I may keep a door in paradise. That I may keep even the smallest door, the furthest, the darkest, coldest door, the door that is least used, the stiffest door. If so it be but in thine house, O God, if so be that I can see thy glory even afar, and hear thy voice O God, and know that I am with thee, thee O God."[132]

THE CHURCH FACING RUIN

Nonetheless, despite those successes, the 500 years now before us were the darkest in the history of the church. They finally did lead to a new period of astonishing growth; but there were times during this half-millennium when there seemed to be a real prospect that Christianity would be overwhelmed by the forces ranged against it.

Not only was the church crushed in all the lands that Islam later overwhelmed, but it seemed possible that Christianity might actually vanish altogether from the earth.

The enemies of the church were both external and internal, and it was often difficult to determine which was the worst foe:

- ➢ in the east, the church remained unified under the protection of the Eastern Roman Emperor, whose capital was now actually Constantinople[133], a great city built on seven hills overlooking the narrow strait that separates European from Asian Turkey, the Bosporus.

- ➢ the southern section (Syria, Egypt, Africa), along with Spain, fell under Muslim control, and those lands were virtually lost to Christendom; a remnant of the church survived, but it has ever since remained a small minority.

- ➢ and in the west, the splintered Germanic kingdoms that arose out of the ruins of the Western Roman Empire were eventually united under the restored Holy Roman Empire; but a savage contest for supremacy soon developed between the new emperors and the popes.

---

132 The Oxford Book of Prayer, ed. George Appleton; Oxford University Press, Oxford; 1985; Selection #492; pg. 145.
133 The city is today called Istanbul.

EXTERNAL FOES

ISLAM

The greatest external threat the church faced during this period was Islam, the religion created and proclaimed by Mahomet, who claimed that he had been commissioned by the angel Gabriel. In response, he called himself the Prophet, and declared that there was only one God, whose name was Allah.[134] The sayings of Mahomet were collected after his death and placed in the Koran (which means "The Recitation"). this volume became the holy book of Islam (which means "Submission" - that is, to Allah).

Within a century of Mahomet's death (in 632), Arab armies bearing the crescent symbol of Islam had carved an empire extending from Spain to India, and were threatening to engulf the entire Mediterranean world. Indeed, at that point Arabs were ruling half of the former territories of the Roman Empire, and had absorbed more than half of the total number of Christians, the majority of whom converted to Islam - many voluntarily, the rest under compulsion.

What do Muslims believe? Why did they gain such huge successes over formerly Christian people and lands?

THE ISLAMIC CREED

Mahomet was strongly influenced by both Christian and Jewish thought (indeed, Islam has often been described as a Christian sect), but he fused those ideas with other elements to form a unique and powerful faith. Much of the moral and ethical teaching of the Koran is drawn from the Hebrew and Christian scriptures, so even from the Christian viewpoint there is much in Muslim teaching that is true.

---

134 Arabic for "The Supreme Being", equivalent to our word "God".

The six "pillars" of Islam, which are incumbent upon every sane male from puberty (about 15 years of age) onward are:

- worship Allah as the sole God
- face Mecca and pray, five times each day
- make at least one pilgrimage to Mecca
- be generous in giving alms
- fast from sunrise to sunset throughout the month of Ramadan
- be willing to sacrifice your life in a holy war.

The Koran is reckoned to be an infallible guide, not only for personal faith and morals, but also for civil law. Many passages in the Koran read much like scripture, and many of the doctrines are the same: the oneness of God; scorn of idolatry; noble moral and ethical strictures; the spiritual nature of men and women; the resurrection of the dead; the coming Day of Judgment; and so on. Jesus is mentioned in the Koran more than twenty times, always with honour, and Islam insists that unless one submits to Christ no salvation is possible. Here, for example, are a few such passages -

THE KORAN ON JESUS AND OTHER THEMES

> "The faithful say, We believe in God, and in the revelation he has given to us, to Abraham, Ishmael, Isaac, Jacob, and to the Tribes. We believe also in the revelation given to Moses and Jesus, and in the revelation given to all the Prophets by their Lord" (2:136).

> "It is God who has sent down to you the Law of Moses and the Gospel of Jesus ... to be a guide to all peoples" (3:3).

> "(God) sent Jesus the son of Mary to confirm the Law that came before him. (He was) sent with the Gospel, wherein is guidance, instruction, and

confirmation of the Law that came before him. In these things all who fear God will find direction and admonition" (5:49).

"Jesus is a Sign, pointing to the coming Day of Judgment. Therefore never doubt that the hour will come, but follow your God, for that is the only pure way" (43:61).

And here is a passage dealing with the Day of Resurrection and of Judgment. There are several others like it in the Koran, which speak truly to the human spirit, and tend to provoke sensitive readers to righteousness

"Your Lord does not forget. He is the Lord of the heavens and the earth and all that is between them. Worship him, then, and be loyal in his service; for is there any other god like him?

'What!' says man, 'When I am once dead, shall I be raised to life?'

"Does man forget that We created him out of the void? ... (Therefore) We will deliver those who fear Us, but the wrongdoers shall be left to endure (the) torments (of hell) upon their knees ...

"There is none in the heavens or on earth but shall return to God in utter submission. He has kept strict count of all his creatures, and one by one they shall approach him on the Day of Resurrection. He will cherish those who accepted the true faith and were charitable in their life-time ...

"Fixed is the Day of Judgment. On that day the Trumpet shall be sounded and you shall come in multitudes. The gates of heaven shall swing open and the mountains shall pass away and become like vapour. Hell will lie in ambush, a home for the transgressors. There they shall abide long ages;

there they shall taste neither refreshment nor any drink, save boiling water and decaying filth: a fitting recompense ... We shall say: `Taste this: you shall have nothing but mounting torment! ... '

"As for the righteous, they shall surely triumph. Theirs shall be gardens and vineyards ... a truly overflowing cup."[135]

Much of the Koran either repeats or echoes biblical truth, so it is small wonder that it has been able to impel millions of people to accept it as the Word of God, and to find deep inspiration in its pages.

WHY ISLAM TRIUMPHED

The reasons for the rapid conquests gained by the Muslims in what had been largely Christian lands include the following -

There was an austere simplicity in its faith and worship, and in its stern monotheism. Against the superstition, corruption, and downright idolatry that was rampant in much of the church at this time Islam looked like a real improvement. The corrupt, indulgent luxury of many Christians contrasted poorly with the fervour and self-denial of the new Muslims. And there were other faults in the church: illiterate Christians had decayed the doctrine of the Trinity into a concept of three separate gods; images and relics were widely venerated; even among the clergy and bishops morals were lax.

Unlike other religions, the nature of the church is such that it cannot survive a serious loss from the purity of life and strictness of doctrine enjoined in the scriptures. When Christians fall away from the standards God requires, divine judgment must inevitably follow, even to God allowing that part of his church to be purged

---

[135] See Sura 19:66,67,72,93-96; 38:49-52,55-57; 78:17-26,30-34. The latter selections were translated by N.J.Dawood; The Koran - With Notes; Penguin Classics, London, 1980.

off the earth. This was certainly part of the reason for Islam's unhindered sweep out of Arabia and across a vast expanse of formerly Christian territory.

Islam had no priesthood, which appealed to people who were already beginning to weary of the oppressions of corrupt bishops, their extortions, their lasciviousness, their arrogant pomp.

The invaders offered rapid promotion, almost limitless booty, and great power to those who joined their ranks. Inevitably, many who had formerly been without hope, or low in the social hierarchy, seized this opportunity for rapid advancement. Paupers became princes, the weak found themselves crushing monarchs, untold wealth poured into the hands of the impoverished, the Islamic tidal wave seemed unstoppable and caught up millions in its exciting advance.

The western Roman Empire was largely in ruins and unable to help its friends in Africa, while the eastern empire, though still sound, was exhausted by centuries of warfare with the Persians; so it too was unable to offer any real resistance to the foe. Hence Christendom had to accept the loss of all Africa, Egypt, Syria, Palestine, and those parts of Arabia that had been penetrated by the gospel. The Persians, equally exhausted, were also overrun, and their ancient Zarathustrian faith almost destroyed.

Though many of the conquered lands had been nominally Christian, the majority of the people were not members of the Catholic church, but of such groups as the Monophysites. The Roman emperors, both west and east, and the Catholic bishops, for decades had often tried to force them back into the orthodox fold either by taxing or persecuting them. Therefore the common people tended to welcome the Arabs as liberators from harsh oppression. The Arabs were also fellow Semites, in contrast with the Greek and Latin overlords of the remnants of the empire, so there was an ethnic bond that made it easier for the people to swap masters.

The Muslims for a long time did not overtly persecute the Christians, so they did not provoke any strong revolt. Indeed, the Koran itself teaches Muslims to treat Christians and Jews with respect, since they too are "people of the Book" (that is, the Bible). However, Muslim culture did confine the church within a mass of regulations, which eventually stifled all real life and growth. So within Muslim lands the Christians steadily decayed into a small minority, which they still remain, and some branches of the church vanished altogether.

THE FLOOD STEMMED

By the beginning of the 8th century, it seemed that Islam might overrun all Europe. Spain had fallen, the Muslims were pushing into France, and were threatening to overthrow even glorious Constantinople, with its host of splendid palaces, magnificent churches, immense wealth and splendid culture. But in the west some able popes gained power (notably the aptly named leonine Leo III), who by skilful diplomacy and sometimes force of arms began to weaken the Islamic advance. Their efforts were sealed by the great victory Charles Martel gained over the Muslims, near Tours in central France, in 732.

Martel was king over the Franks, the people who preceded modern France and Germany. If the Arabs had won that crucial battle, Europe may well have followed North Africa and become wholly Muslim. The Mediterranean, as someone has said, would now be an Arab lake, and Christianity may have been exterminated, or at best have struggled on as a tiny minority.[136]

---

136 We face a similar threat in our time, for Islam is unquestionably the most virulent foe against which the church must contend. Presently there are about one billion Muslims in the world, which represents a 500% growth in the past 50 years. During the same period, the church has grown about 50%, to about two billion people. In the world also there are some 500 million Hindus, 250 million Buddhists, and 20 million Jews.

Here then is a disturbing thought: apart from Spain, the church has never been able to regain any territory once it was captured by Islam (and even in Spain the land was re-captured for the church 500 years later only by force of arms). Islam, with the Koran, its monotheism, its stern ethic, its simple rules, is immensely appealing to spiritual minds. It is in many ways so close to Christianity that gospel preaching has seldom made any inroads into Muslim culture, whereas Islam, with its freedom to use violence, finds it easy to subdue a decadent church.[137]

Despite the havoc it had wreaked, Islam had a profound influence upon the church, especially in the west.

Two important long-term aspects of that influence were -

THE LONG-TERM INFLUENCE OF ISLAM

CULTURAL ENRICHMENT

As Islam advanced into Asia Minor and Greece, conquering ever more of the territory of the Byzantine (or Eastern Roman) Empire, a growing stream of scholars fled to western Europe, carrying with them the magnificent literature, art, learning, and culture, of the ancient Greek world. Much of this had been lost to the west, following the collapse of the western empire. Indeed, Europe had subsided into a Dark Age, and was now only half-civilised. But the rediscovery of the knowledge amassed over the centuries by the old Greeks and Romans led to a new flowering of scholarship in Europe. The eventual result of that flowering was the marvellous explosion of learning and art that we call the Renaissance. For 500 years Islam had displayed a more civilised culture than could be found anywhere in Europe. But now,

---

[137] I do not mean that Christians have lacked violence in their own methods. The sorry story of the Crusades is enough to show that "Christian" cruelty has sometimes equalled the worst Muslim excesses. But the true church of Jesus Christ cannot be built by any method other than love. Whatever so-called Christianity results from bloodshed and rapine is a sham.

beginning with the Renaissance, Europe soon outstripped Islamic achievements in every field, while the Muslim lands slowly decayed.

CRUSADER ENTERPRISE

The transfer of culture begun by the flight of the Greek scholars was enhanced by the comings and goings of the Crusader armies from the 11th to the 14th centuries. The first Crusaders, who were mostly illiterate (and proud of it), were staggered by the splendours they discovered in Muslim lands. They soon adopted the finest aspects of Islamic culture themselves, and began to carry it back to their homelands. Courtly manners, elegant furnishings, a new appreciation of poetry, more sophisticated music, began to blossom from England to Italy. The dark shadows of ignorance and squalor began to fade away from European society; the way was being prepared for the Renaissance, but far more importantly (from a Christian viewpoint), for the Reformation. The Protestant revolution fractured western society and sundered the mediaeval church, but it also unleashed a surging spiritual and social dynamic that still reverberates around the world.

BARBARIANS

THE FALL OF ROME

The last Western Roman Emperor was the pitiful Romulus Augustulus, who reigned for only a few months, and then in 476 was thrown off his throne by the Germanic mercenary Odoacer. That final collapse of imperial power opened the way for a seemingly endless tide of barbarians to flood into Europe from every quarter. They inflicted terrible ruin upon Roman art and culture, they ravaged the buildings and statuary of the fallen empire, they tore apart its social and political structures. The great force that had brought cohesion and general peace to the Mediterranean world for a thousand years was no more.

Yet surprisingly, the barbarian threat to the church was more apparent than real, for although they brought prodigious disruption and much suffering (rape, robbery, enslavement) to the Roman populace, their pagan creeds and gods were no match for the gospel. So the barbarians were soon converted - at least nominally. There were many occasions when entire tribes, even nations, converted overnight at the command of a prince or military leader.

THE EXAMPLE OF BONIFACE

Consider, for example, the English missionary Boniface, who crossed the Channel in 718, believing he was called by God to preach the gospel to the pagan tribes of central Germany. He enjoyed huge success, attracted enormous crowds, and baptised multitudes of people in great outdoor ceremonies. He was made a bishop in 723, and archbishop in 732, but ten years later, tiring of pomp and high office, resigned his seat and went back to pioneer mission work. A few months later, once again reaping a harvest of souls, he was about to baptise a group of new converts in a river when a group of envious pagans fell upon him and beat him to death. He was then about 80 years of age, and he died, not defending himself, but clutching a copy of the gospels. Perhaps his most famous act occurred when he was challenged to prove that the Christian God was greater than Thor, the lord of the northmen. Boniface took an axe and cut down a huge oak tree, one that was sacred to the pagan god, then used the timber to build a Christian chapel. When no harm came to the missionary, thousands forsook Thor and clamoured for Christian baptism.

MASS BAPTISMS

The kind of mass baptism practised by Boniface and others is often viewed with suspicion by modern evangelicals. But judging by the missionaries and monks, the priests and bishops, who quickly rose out of those same tribes, a surprising number of the conversions must have been genuine. Consider the case of King Boris of Bulgaria, who ruled a pagan state in the 9th Century. Somewhere around 865 Boris decided to become a Christian. His motives were mixed: partly fright, induced by seeing some pictures of hell painted on a wall by a monk;[138] partly as a jest; partly for political reasons - he wanted an alliance with the Byzantine Emperor. Many of his pagan nobles revolted against this change of religion and tried to unthrone Boris, but they were ruthlessly suppressed. He then invited monks to come into his land and teach his people. Since they were supported by royal patronage their labours were

---

[138] In former times a painting could produce the same effect on viewers as a moving film may do upon us. Here is a quaint example from 10th century Japan -

"On the day after the Naming of the Buddhas the screens with the
(Continued on the next page)

(Continued from previous page....   )

paintings of Hell were carried into the Empress' apartments for her to see. They were terrifying beyond words.

"'Look!' said Her Majesty. But I replied that I had no desire to see them; I was so frightened that I went and lay down in my room next door where I could hide myself from the screens.

"It was raining very hard. Since the Emperor declared that he was bored, some of the senior courtiers were summoned to the Empress' apartments for a concert. Michikata, the Minor Counsellor, played splendidly on the lute, Lord Narimasa played the thirteen-string zither, Yukinari the ordinary flute, and Captain Tsunefusa the thirteen-pipe flute. They gave a delightful performance of one piece; then, after the sound of the flute had stopped, His Excellency the Major Counsellor, Korechika, chanted the line,

'The music stops, but the player will not speak her name.'

"While all this was going on, I lay out of sight in my room; but now I got up and went into the Empress' apartments. 'Whatever guilt this may bring upon me,' I said as I entered, 'I cannot resist such a charming recitation.' Hearing this, the gentlemen all burst out laughing.

"I recall that there was nothing very remarkable about the Major Counsellors' voice; yet it seemed to have been made especially for the occasion."

(From The Pillow Book of Sei Shonagon; tr. by Ivan Morris; Penguin Classics, 1967; page 87; selection # 50. Sei Shonagon was a lady-in-waiting at the imperial court of 10th-century Japan.)

crowned with uncommon success, and multitudes of Bulgarians were converted and baptised. Churches sprang up everywhere, schools and seminaries were established, and soon native Bulgarians were being ordained and assuming ever higher leadership roles in the burgeoning faith. Boris even sent his younger son, Prince Simeon, to Constantinople to be trained as a priest, hoping that he might eventually become the primate of Bulgaria.

So for 25 years the church in Bulgaria flourished and expanded. King Boris then decided to retire to a monastery, to spend his remaining years in prayer, and he placed his older son Vladimir on the throne. But the young man reverted to paganism and began to persecute the church. For a few years Boris kept hoping for a change of heart; but when his son proved obdurate he suddenly emerged furious from his monastery, arrested Vladimir, put out both his eyes, threw him into prison, and placed his younger brother Simeon on the throne. With the kingdom at peace again, and the church advancing once more, Boris retired to his monastery and his prayers, and died there a few years later, satisfied that God would reward him well for his efforts[139]!

THE RISE OF THE CHURCH

The fall of the western empire, though it brought fearful upheaval and awful distress to the people, strangely had little ill effect on the church. On the contrary, the church gained strength, amidst the fragmentation of the Roman world, from its tightly knit structures, and its single government, headed (in the west) by the pope. So long as the emperor had reigned in Rome, the pope was overshadowed; but when the last emperor was forced to abdicate, and the throne was vacant, suddenly the pope (the bishop of Rome) became the most visible figure in the western world. No other

---

[139] See A History of the Expansion of Christianity, vol 2, pg 241 ff; by K. S. Latourette.

ruler remotely equalled him in the extent of his authority, which stretched from the distant British Isles in the west to the very borders of Byzantium in the east. The church remained the one coherent organisation in a ruined world.

The church also gained because its organisational structure duplicated that of the secular empire, with its parishes, dioceses, and the like, and even in the titles of its many functionaries.[140] So when the secular officials abandoned their offices it was easy for church dignitaries, who often bore the same or similar titles, and ruled over mostly the same districts, to step in and take control. The people did not resent this; on the contrary, it was welcomed as a sign of stability and sanity in a world that was full of terror. So the fall of pagan Rome inevitably led to the rise of Christian Rome, and the western church steadily increased its prestige and power.

Let me close this chapter with the comment that the ready conversion of the heathen showed that while it is easy for a "high" religion to supplant a "low" one, the reverse has never been known to happen. It is even difficult for one "high" religion to compete successfully with another (cp. the failure of the church to convert the Jews). Apart from the early Muslim advances, there is no record in history of such a thing happening; but as we have seen, there were special reasons for the initial Arab victories.

Yet one other observation needs to be made: one "high" religion may replace another if the former is in a state of great vitality while the latter is in a state of decadence. Thus it is remarkable, in our time, to see Islam and Hinduism advancing in nominally Christian countries, while the gospel is advancing in Asia and even in some parts of the Muslim world!

---

[140] In much the same way as the Salvation Army in our day has copied the structure and titles of the secular armed forces.

Chapter Nine:
PAPAL ASCENDANCY

INTRODUCTION

"(Lord Arthur Savile) wandered across Oxford Street into narrow, shameful alleys. Two women with painted faces mocked him as he went by. From a dark courtyard came a sound of oaths and blows, followed by shrill screams, and, huddled upon a damp door-step, he saw the crooked-back forms of poverty. ... A strange pity came over him. Were these children of sin and misery pre-destined to their end, as he to his? Were they, like him, merely the puppets of a monstrous show?

"And yet it was not the mystery, but the comedy of suffering that struck him; its absolute uselessness, its grotesque want of meaning. How incoherent everything seemed! How lacking in all harmony! He was amazed at the discord between the shallow optimism of the day and the real facts of existence." [141]

Anyone contemplating the entire canvas of life, or looking back across the pages of history, and banishing God from the picture, must come to the same sort of conclusion as did the worthy peer. It looks like a mess of senseless confusion. Why was the church allowed to fall so far? Why was Islam allowed to rise so high? What about the millions of

---

[141] Oscar Wilde, <u>Lord Arthur Savile's Crime</u>, Ch. Two.

helpless people who still suffer so barbarically in endless persecutions, wars, civil strife, famines, floods, fires, pestilences? How is it possible to see any purpose or guiding hand in it all?

> Tomorrow, and tomorrow, and tomorrow,
>
> Creeps in this petty pace from day to day,
>
> To the last syllable of recorded time;
>
> And all our yesterdays have lighted fools
>
> The way to dusty death. Out, out, brief candle!
>
> Life's but a walking shadow, a poor player
>
> That struts and frets his hour upon the stage,
>
> And then is heard no more; it is a tale
>
> Told by an idiot, full of sound and fury,
>
> Signifying nothing. [142]

JESUS: THE KEY TO HISTORY

Well, of course, apart from scripture and the revelation faith grasps, it is not possible. The Bible itself is a picture of that principle. Consider Israel: purportedly called out of Egypt by God, yet soon broken into two endlessly warring kingdoms. Good monarchs reign a few years; foul kings occupy the throne for decades. Conquerors and despots come and go, seemingly at will. The poor cry for justice, and are the more despoiled; the weak cry for protection, and are the more violated. The two kingdoms are ultimately destroyed and carried off to slavery in a distant land, and only a remnant of one of them is ever able to return to the land of their fathers, the land of Promise. Some promise! On the surface it seems like some sort of hideous, mocking, comedy.

---

[142] William Shakespeare, McBeth, Act V, Sc. v.

With seemingly good reason, as the psalmist acknowledged, the heathen derided Israel: "Where is your God?" (Ps 115:1-2). Yet the psalmist could not help but affirm: "Our God is in heaven, and he does whatever he pleases!"

That is a statement of faith. It can be made only by someone who has captured the revelation of scripture and is therefore able to discern the hand of God at work through all the broiling, turbulent, conflicting currents of life. Look at any one decade, or even year, and it may often seem that God is even more the victim of circumstance than we are. But gaze across twenty centuries, and everywhere the hand of the Almighty can be seen at work, directing human freedom of choice toward the ultimate fulfilment of his own divine purpose for his church. As Ernest Renan said: "The whole of history is incomprehensible without Jesus!"[143]

In that sense the study of history is not merely an academic pursuit. It has great meaning for our own time and for each person's own life. As surely as I know that the Father has guided his church across the stormy seas of two millennia, so I know he will keep me safely through the decades of my own life, and bring me in his time to the heavenly shore.

So let us resume our story. The fifth century has ended. The sixth is about to begin -

THE BEGINNING OF THE SIXTH CENTURY

A NEW ERA

By the beginning of the 6th century the basic structure of the church was established on the pattern still followed by the Roman Catholic and Orthodox churches (plus some others). That is,

---

[143] French essayist and historian (1823-1892); from the "Introduction" to his Life of Jesus (1863).

- the distinction between priests and bishops was firmly maintained;
- the bishops now had authority over large areas and many churches;
- there was no church without the bishop, and no salvation without the church;
- the apostolic succession[144] of the bishops was firmly believed;
- the clergy were thought of as "priests", acting as intermediaries between God and the ordinary people;[145]
- the government of the church was divided between five bishops (Alexandria, Jerusalem, Antioch, Constantinople, Rome), with the pope ever more loudly claiming to be "the first among equals" while pressing toward an absolute primacy.

That claim, and the reasons for it, are the next part of our study.

THE DEVELOPMENT OF THE PAPAL CLAIMS

AN ABSOLUTE PRIMACY

The papal claim to primacy over the entire church (both west and east) was based upon several foundations, some of them reasonable, some of them fallacious. They were -

the belief that Paul and Peter founded the church in Rome; a belief that can be held only as an article of faith, for it has no sound historical foundation.

---

144 That is, the belief that there is an unbroken succession of ordination from the apostles to the bishops of the present day.

145 Thus the Roman Catholic Church today sees the clergy as priests who bring the people to God; whereas the Protestant Reformers saw the clergy as prophets who bring God to the people.

the belief that Peter was the chief of the apostles, and that the bishops of Rome were the only ones who could prove an unbroken succession of ordination from Peter - once again, both of those propositions are historically unsustainable.

the greater prestige the pope gained from ruling all of the western empire, while the four other patriarchs had to share the smaller territory of the eastern empire between them.

the declining prestige of pagan Rome as a political power, which tended to enhance the pope's prestige, not only religiously, but also politically, administratively, and socially. By contrast, the nearest rival to the pope, the patriarch of Constantinople, had to dwell under the shadow of the emperor, a situation that continued for another thousand years.

the fact that when the western empire collapsed, the pope was the only figure whose authority was recognised everywhere. Although he could do little to prevent the overthrow of the empire, the unifying influence of the pope helped to prevent the total demise of European civilisation.

POPE LEO THE GREAT

There were also several occasions when the popes were instrumental in saving Rome itself from being devastated by invaders; sometimes by gathering armies together, sometimes by diplomacy. The story of Pope Leo I, The Great (c. 450) well illustrates the role the popes often had to take. He was one of the ablest of the popes, and twice saved Rome from being ravaged. The first occasion was in 452, when by bribery and persuasion he convinced Attila the Hun to cancel his plans to attack and pillage Rome. Then, only three years later, he turned aside the armies of Genseric the Vandal who had vowed to kill every man, woman, and child in the defenceless city. Leo persuaded Genseric to spare the lives of the people, but he had to agree to allow the invading army 14 days of unhindered sacking of Rome and its suburbs. The people stood by helpless, enraged, weeping, as their city was looted and their wealth plundered. Little wonder the name of Vandal became one of the most pejorative words in our tongue.

Leo was a key figure in establishing papal supremacy in the west. He argued vigorously for the doctrine that Peter had conveyed his authority primarily to the bishops of Rome, and he intervened so successfully in a doctrinal dispute, that even the eastern bishops were constrained to say, "Peter has spoken through Leo" - fateful words, that later popes did not hesitate to use in pressing their claim that all other bishops should submit to them.

POPE VERSUS PATRIARCH

Papal supremacy was given a boost from time to time because it often suited the emperor in Constantinople to recognise the authority of the pope. This placed the patriarch in an inferior position. Unlike the advantage the pope was gaining in the west, the decay of the eastern empire did not bring any enhancement of the patriarch's power. Although he alone survived the Muslim onslaught, after the lands ruled by the patriarchs of Alexandria, Jerusalem, and Antioch had come under an Islamic yoke, it meant only that he now spoke against the pope with one voice instead of four. And even that one voice was overshadowed by the still dominant authority of the emperor.

The patriarch's voice was often muted also because of the volatile nature of the churches over which he ruled. The passionate Greeks were much given to controversy, and were frequently torn apart by heated arguments.

But in the west, while Roman Catholic structures had departed far from the simple pattern of the early church, her doctrines had remained comparatively orthodox and stable. The western churches were therefore still aggressively evangelistic in their outlook, driven by an urgent desire to convert the many pagan tribes that were still unreached with the gospel. Those missionary efforts were crowned with success and many barbarian communities converted to Christianity en masse. They naturally looked to the pope as a central and strong figure.

Clovis the Frank and his followers are a notable example of that process. His wife Clotilda was a Burgundian princess, and a Catholic, who kept trying to persuade her husband to adopt the Christian faith. She gained her heart's desire when Clovis found himself on the edge of defeat in battle, and called upon his wife's God, promising to become a Christian if he won. The tide of war turned, Clovis gained a notable triumph, and kept his promise to God and to Clotilda. He was baptised on Christmas Day, 496, along with thousands of his people. He went on to conquer most of Gaul, made his capital at Paris, and laid the foundations of a state that for the next four centuries would be the most powerful in western Europe, and came eventually to be called -

THE HOLY ROMAN EMPIRE

The influence of the Frankish state across the ensuing centuries, especially in the spread of Christianity across the remainder of northern and central Europe (which was then still pagan), was enormous. Indeed, from the time of Clovis' baptism the church in the west had to look for its defence, not to the enfeebled emperors in Constantinople, but to the powerful kings of the Franks, along with other strong Germanic princes. Those rulers, in their turn, sought to stabilise their kingdoms, to authenticate their sometimes bloodily purchased thrones, and to add to their prestige, by seeking support from the popes. Thus a mutual dependency was formed between prince and bishop, emperor and pope.

In the 8th century, for example, the Frankish general Charles Martel was a strong supporter of the popes and a thoroughly orthodox Christian, who fought several battles on the pope's behalf. His son and successor Pepin was anointed king of the Franks by the pope,[146] thus foreshadowing the time when the pope would actually crown triumphant Charlemagne (in 800) as emperor

---

146 Pepin also gave the pope large tracts of land, of which only the territories of the Vatican now remain.

over what began to be called the Holy Roman Empire. In turn, the pope (Leo III) knelt in temporal homage before the emperor. He had good reason to do so, for he owed his life to Charlemagne. He had clawed his way to the papal throne, and had to contend with many enemies, including the friends of a rival claimant to the tiara. They once seized Leo and tried to blind him and to cut out his tongue. But with Charlemagne's help he managed to escape unscathed, which was thought by his contemporaries to be a miracle, and established him as a prelate favoured by God.

A NEW ALLIANCE

With the crowning of Charlemagne by Leo a new kind of alliance was forged between the church and the state. In fact, many people of that time thought that a golden era, perhaps even the kingdom of God, had arrived! The emperor gained his authority from the pope; and the pope depended upon the emperor for temporal support. They were supposed to be equals, having authority in different areas, but the idea seldom worked; subsequent emperors and popes often contended bitterly with each other for supreme power in each other's realms.

The Holy Roman Empire itself is reckoned to have begun officially with the crowning of the German prince Otto I in 962. He established an empire which endured, with varying fortunes and in ever-changing relationship with the papacy, for 850 years.

This concept of the Holy Roman Empire as a kind of Christian successor to the old pagan empire, although it endured for so long, was a source of endless conflict. Various ambitious rulers endlessly marched their armies across Europe in an effort to establish themselves as the heirs of the Caesars, or else to resist the vaulting ambitions of a prince who wished to be Caesar. The terrible Thirty-years' War was part of these constant battles, which were marked by dreadful savagery, havoc, and bloodshed. That particular war, however, did have one useful result: the violence had been so unrestrained that it forever after gave religious bigotry a foul name, and the first real efforts were begun toward religious toleration.

The Holy Roman Empire was finally abolished by Napoleon Bonaparte in 1806.[147] He also reversed the precedent set by Charlemagne, for when the pope was about to crown him Napoleon seized the crown and placed it upon his own head. Thus he showed his scorn of the pope's claim to possess a higher power.

THE DAYS OF GLORY

The authority and prestige of the papacy reached a high point during the lifetime of Charlemagne, whose dominions included nearly all of central and western Europe, excluding Spain and southern Italy. Many legends grew up around Charlemagne. The apostles Peter and Paul were supposed to have appeared to him and given him the standard, under which he fought, and which was thought to be the source of his astonishing triumphs. It was said also (probably falsely) that he had an unnatural love for his sister, which he did not dare to confess. But the king's behaviour, written on a scroll in a vision, was revealed by an angel to a hermit by the name of St Giles. As the saint interceded for the monarch, the words on the scroll slowly vanished, and the king was pardoned. The saint nonetheless called upon him to abandon all sin and to serve righteousness.

St Giles himself was a Greek who decided he was called by God to a solitary life. So he moved to a forest in France, and there lived alone for many years, with a deer as his only companion. This deer had taken refuge with the hermit when it was being pursued by hunters. St Giles was struck by an arrow intended for the beast, which left him a cripple. Consequently he became the patron saint of cripples, which is why around the world various hospitals for the infirm are named after him.

---

147 Some historians, however, believe that Kaiser Wilhelm and Adolf Hitler were both of them moved in part by the ancient dream of setting up again the throne of the Caesars.

After Charlemagne's death, his empire began to crumble into the numerous warring states that characterised mediaeval Europe. As they struggled against each other, they also resisted the claims of the Holy Roman Emperor to suzerainty over them all, which eroded the power of the imperial throne. This decline of the Holy Roman Empire adversely affected the influence of the popes, who were also distracted by the Viking inroads in the north and west, by renewed Muslim attacks from the south, and by the onslaughts of the Huns and other barbarians from the east.

Some of the popes even had to raise their own armies in order to protect Rome: for example, John VIII, who spent most of his pontificate defending Rome and Italy against the Saracens. On one occasion he was forced (when the Saracen armies were almost at the gates of Rome) to agree to pay them an annual tribute. Later he was assassinated in his own palace (in 882) by members of his household, who had been bribed by some of his political and religious foes.

THE GREATEST POPE

Gregory I, The Great (590-604) was possibly the greatest of all the popes. He was outstanding in piety, learning, orthodoxy, charity, character, and administrative skills. Born into a wealthy family, he was trained in law and in Roman civil administration, but he gave away his riches, abandoned a promising political career, and became a monk. His life was so radiant that three of his aunts dedicated themselves as virgins, and two of them were later canonised. His widowed mother entered a convent, and she too was later canonised.

He founded several monasteries, served the church well as a diplomat, and was finally himself called to the papal throne, which at first, because he was frail and often ill, he refused. But being told in a vision to accept the office he resigned himself to the inevitable.

Although Gregory faced enormous problems, and complained to God about "the rotten old ship of which you have made me captain", he virtually completed by himself the process of Romanising the western church. With him the papacy finally gained effective and permanent control over all the churches in Europe, a control that was not seriously threatened for nearly a thousand years. Within his lifetime, though, he twice had to raise an army to drive back the Lombards. They were a Hungarian people who invaded Italy and established a strong kingdom. Their expansion was finally stopped by Charlemagne, and in the 11th century they were destroyed by the Normans. But for a while they added greatly to the burdens Gregory had to carry.

During his short pontificate of only 14 years, Gregory "more than any other man, laid the foundations for the power which the Church of Rome was to exercise in western Europe for the next nine centuries" (Latourette). Among other things, Pope Gregory was responsible for

- changing and standardising both the calendar and the liturgy throughout the west (he probably did not invent the Gregorian Chant, but he certainly standardised it).
- endorsing (no doubt sincerely) many elements of popular piety (such as reverence for the relics of the saints) that we would today consider superstition (but we have our own varieties).
- putting tradition upon an equal footing with scripture.
- formalising the doctrine of purgatory, a fire in which Christians are purged of light sins as a preparation for the final judgment.
- commending the idea that masses said for the souls of the dead might help them escape purgatory more quickly.
- systematising the popular doctrines of angels and demons, and fixing hierarchies for both.

- ➢ formalising the doctrine of the Eucharist as a sacrifice performed by the priest.
- ➢ approving the invocation of saints and martyrs, and believing rather credulously in many miracles.
- ➢ promoting asceticism and enforcing celibacy for the clergy.
- ➢ encouraging missionary zeal, and sending out many monks and missionaries (especially to Britain).
- ➢ appropriating the title "servant of the servants of God" (which Gregory might not have meant in the way it was taken by later popes).[148]
- ➢ enforcing his authority over all other bishops (especially in the west).
- ➢ proclaiming the imminent end of the world.

The Venerable Bede tells a charming story about him -

> "I must here relate a story handed down to us by the tradition of our forbears, which explains Gregory's deep desire for the salvation of our (English) nation.
>
> "We are told that one day some merchants who had recently arrived in Rome displayed their many wares in the market-place. Among the crowds who thronged to buy was Gregory, who saw among the other merchandise some boys exposed for sale. These had fair complexions, fine-cut features, and beautiful hair. Looking at them with interest, he enquired from what country and what part of the world they came. 'They come from the island of

---

[148] They used it to enforce their authority; but Gregory may have been intending to shame the bishops. Gregory had asked them: "Do you call yourselves the rulers or the servants of the people?" They dared not say other than "servants". So he said: "As you are the servants of the people, so am I your servant!

Britain,' he was told, 'where all the people have this appearance.' He then asked whether the islanders were Christians, or whether they were still ignorant heathens. 'They are pagans,' he was informed. 'Alas!' said Gregory with a heartfelt sigh, 'how sad that such bright-faced folk are still in the grip of the author of darkness, and that such graceful features conceal minds void of God's grace! What is the name of this race?' 'They are called Angles,' he was told. 'That is appropriate,' he said, 'for they have angelic faces, and it is right that they should become joint-heirs with the angels in heaven!'"[149]

On the imminence of Christ's return Gregory spoke with great passion and urgency -

> "What is there now, I ask you, which might give pleasure in this world? Everywhere we see grief, on all sides we hear groans. Cities are destroyed, armed camps overturned, districts emptied of people, the earth reduced to solitude. ...

> "What is there then in this life, my brothers, that might give pleasure. If we still love such a world, we now love wounds, not delights. ...

> "What we have said about the destruction of the city of Rome we see in all the cities of the world. Some places are desolated through slaughter, others consumed by the sword, others tortured by famine, others swallowed up by clefts in the earth. Let us despise with all our being this present - or rather

---

[149] The slaves were young men from what we now call Yorkshire. Gregory later sent Augustine to evangelise the British. From <u>Ecclesiastical History of the English People</u>, by the Venerable Bede (673-675); tr. by Leo Sherley-Price; Penguin Classics, London, 1990; Book (II)(1); pg. 103.

extinct - world. At least let worldly desires end with the End of the world."[150]

"Further, we also wish Your Majesty to know, as we have learned from the words of Almighty God in Holy Scripture, that the End of the present world is already near, and that the unending kingdom of the Saints is approaching. As this same End of the world is drawing nigh, many unusual things will happen - climatic changes, terrors from heaven, unseasonable tempests, wars, famines, pestilences, earthquakes. ... If you are aware of some of them happening in your land, do not be disturbed, for these signs of the End of the world are sent ahead so that we may have a concern for our souls. Awaiting the hour of death, by our good actions may we be found ready for the Judge who is to come."[151]

---

150 From a Homily on Ezekiel 2:6. <u>Visions of the End - Apocalyptic traditions in the Middle Ages</u>, by Bernard McGinn; Columbia University Press, New York, 1979; pg. 63,63.

151 Ibid. pg. 64. From a Letter to Ethelbert, King of the Angles (June 601). McGinn makes the ironic comment that "one whose influence was to have such pronounced effect on the future of Western society did not think that that society had any future at all."

Chapter Ten:
PAPAL DESCENDENCY

We have seen the papacy rise to splendour. Now we see its sad nadir.

During the 9th and 10th centuries, although there were several fine popes, the papacy in general slumped to its lowest moral and spiritual level. Some of the popes were driven out of Rome for scandalous behaviour, and wealthy families bought and sold the papal office.

POPE BENEDICT IX

One of the more scurrilous pontiffs was Benedict IX (1032-1045). He was born of noble lineage, with the rank of count. While still a teenager he purchased the papal crown, but held it for only a short time before he was driven out of Rome by the people because of his utterly corrupt character. By the use of many wiles he regained the papacy, then sold it for a profit. Yet once again he manoeuvred his way back onto Peter's chair, and again was driven off it by a scandalised populace. He managed to repeat the process at least once more. Then, determined to regain the office he had sold, he poisoned the pope who succeeded him, and captured the throne, only to be finally deposed by the emperor Henry III. He died twenty years later in a convent (!), and was said to have been deeply penitent!

CRITICAL VOICES

Supporters of the papacy argued (as they still do) that a consecrated bishop remains effective in fulfilling his official functions no matter what his personal character might be.

Protestants inevitably admit the same principle to some extent, [152] but not so thoroughly as do Catholics. Nonetheless, during both high and low points in the papacy, there were always some voices raised against the papal claims. For example, Claudius, bishop of Turin, in the first part of the 9th century,

> "vigorously denounced the reverence of images and of the cross ... He also came out against the current practice of asking for the intercession of the saints. Even more striking was his attitude towards the papacy. He was critical of the pope, declaring that he is not to be called an apostle who sits in the seat of an apostle, but he who does the work of an apostle." [153]

CONTINUED EXPANSION

Surprisingly perhaps, and despite its losses to Islam, the church continued to expand during the 9th and 10th centuries, both in the east and especially in the west. The lands north of the borders of the old Roman Empire were Christianised, along with what is now Poland, Hungary, Norway, Iceland, Sweden, and other lands. That growth, despite the disintegration of Europe and the often decadent state of the papacy, enabled the popes to maintain a great measure of power. Sometimes, indeed, growth was enhanced by both of the former problems:

- ➢ the fragmentation of Europe often allowed the popes to play off one prince against -another, and to gain absolute control over many lesser rulers; and

- ➢ the moral decay of the papacy freed the popes to use whatever means were available to achieve their ends, including bribery, murder, poison, and armed conquest.

---

[152] What Protestant pastor can claim to be without sin?

[153] Latourette, History of Christianity, vol 1, pg 362.

When questions were raised about their sometimes dubious methods, they excused their behaviour by misquoting St Jerome, who once commented (disapprovingly) on "the rule, often adopted by strong men in controversy, of justifying the means by the end" ("Letter # 48"). The popes had two great weapons by which they could enforce their will: excommunication; and interdict.[154] Both weapons gained their strength from two things: (a) a belief that salvation was wholly dependent upon being in good standing with the bishops and the church; and (b) on a superstitious dread of hell, which sat very vividly in the imaginations of people during the Middle Ages.

FURTHER DOCTRINAL DEVELOPMENTS

Toward the end of the period we are considering, the following doctrinal developments occurred -

The idea began to surface, in the face of furious protests, that the elements of the Eucharist became the actual flesh and blood of Christ. This was never an original part of Christian teaching, but by the 13th century it had become official Roman Catholic doctrine.

The idea was first promulgated that God has predestined both the saved to be rescued and the damned to perish. Strangely, this idea

---

154 An "interdict" prohibited access to the sacraments, to Christian marriage, and to burial in sanctified ground, which for most people in those times meant being cut off from salvation and condemned to hell. There were three kinds of interdict:
- personal: which affected only an individual.
- local: which affected a district, town, or village.
- regional: which affected a region, state, or even an entire nation.

Only the pope could impose the third kind of interdict. Theoretically, it is still possible for bishops or popes to issue interdicts, but it would be highly improbable in the present environment.

was finally rejected by the Roman Catholic church, but later became the doctrine of some Protestant churches.

In place of open discipline (such as public confession, exclusion from the eucharist, and a period of probation) the practice began to develop of private confession to a priest, with the priest setting a personal penance and giving priestly absolution. This became standard Catholic practice, but was later rejected by the Protestant churches.

A people already superstitious became even more deeply so, and were disposed naively to accept anything that appeared to be supernatural. So from the 6th century on the writings of bishops and scholars contain far more abundant references to miracles than can be found in those of the previous 500 years.

THE USE OF RELICS

A good example of superstition can be found in the story of an abbot who was a close friend of Charlemagne. He sent agents to Rome, who entered a church, befriended its clergy, and after prayers with them, stole some holy relics of the martyrs, which they proudly conveyed back to the abbot. That cleric then solemnly recorded the many miracles the relics were supposed to have wrought among his people!

Throughout Europe you could find monks and priests carrying relics and displaying them for a fee. Describing the 14th century, Brian H. Edwards writes -

> "Everywhere friars travelled with their holy relics, which, for a fee, could be viewed and kissed. In Germany, in the city of Martin Luther, at Wittenberg in Saxony, the Castle Church contained over 17,000 relics, including part of the rock on which Jesus stood when he wept over Jerusalem, the gown of the Virgin Mary and some milk from her breasts, a piece from the burning bush of Moses, thirty-five portions of the cross, hay and straw from

the manger at Bethlehem, some hair from Christ, his coat and girdle, and even a complete skeleton of one of the babes murdered by Herod at Bethlehem! The Elector of Saxony was proud of his collection. This was an Indulgence Church; the pilgrim could earn 127,709 years and 116 days off purgatory by viewing them all; as a bonus he helped to increase the Church revenues ... "

A hundred years later, in his notes on his Greek New Testament, the great scholar Erasmus wrote this comment on Matthew 23:27:

"What would Jerome say could he see the virgin's milk exhibited for money, with as much honour paid to it as to the consecrated body of Christ; the miraculous oil; the portions of the true cross, enough if they were collected to freight a large ship? Here we have the hood of St Francis, there Our Lady's petticoat, or St Anne's comb, or St Thomas of Canterbury's shoes; not presented as innocent aids to religion, but as the substance of religion itself."[155]

Such absurd delusions darkened the mission of the church for centuries. They were dealt a powerful blow by the 16th century Reformation; yet they are still endemic in many parts of the church around the world.

SOCIETY CHANGED

During the first five centuries, the church had a purity, simplicity, and soundness of doctrine that sharply contrasted with its general state during the next five centuries: nominal mass conversions; high offices bought and sold; bishops living and behaving like feudal lords; illiterate clergy; periods of awful decadence at Rome.

---

155 God's Outlaw; Evangelical Press, 1976; pg. 40, 44.

Yet remarkably, the actual influence of the church in changing at least the outward appearance of society was greater in the second period than it had been in the first. At the end of the first 500 years the face of Roman society was hardly different from what it had been when Christianity came into existence; but by the end of the second period, Europe was thoroughly Christianised in all of its institutions, law, culture, social life, and so on. Both western and eastern Europe now bore the appearance, though not much of the reality, of a Christian society.

THE EASTERN ORTHODOX CHURCHES

THE CHURCH UNDER ISLAM

A STIFLED CHURCH

By the year 1000, the influence of the church in the east was much diminished in relation to that of the western church, which was growing in vitality, wealth, and in political power. The Islamic conquests had removed vast numbers of adherents from the eastern church, and although the church survived in Muslim lands, it was imprisoned behind a multitude of legal and social restraints. What growth it enjoyed came mostly by natural increase, for conversions were usually prohibited. That situation remained basically unchanged until the Protestant missionaries began to penetrate Muslim lands in the 19th century, albeit without much success. However, a newly militant Islam in the 20th century is threatening once again to destroy the churches (both old and new) within its dominions.

By the end of the millennium, even outside Muslim lands, the eastern church found itself obliged to remain defensive. It was confined by its role as an agent of the imperial government, and it lacked the vitality (both for good and ill) that more and more characterised the west. Indeed, the very collapse of the western empire, and the freeing of the churches from their imperial connection, enabled the western church to develop its own administration and doctrines in ways that would have been otherwise impossible.

ICONS AND CONTROVERSIES

The weakening east and the burgeoning west would have seemed most improbable to a 6th century observer. At that time, with the western empire in ruins, and with western society and culture in a state of almost total disruption, it would have seemed far more likely that the future lay with the east. In the 6th century, the east had the largest churches, the greater number of Christians, a stable society, used the language of the NT, and was the centre of most theological learning. But how dramatically all of that was to change during the ensuing 500 years! Which shows how perilous it is to predict either the success or the failure of any particular segment of the church! Only a brave man or a fool would hazard a guess about what shape the church will have a century or two from now! Will it triumph, and eradicate Islam and its other main competitors? Will Islam or one of the eastern religions prevail, so that the church is reduced to a trembling remnant? Will there be a great revival, sweeping across the planet, carrying millions of people into the kingdom of God? Will there be a tragic falling away, so that when Jesus comes he will hardly be able to find faith on the earth (Luke 18:8)? Only God knows!

WHY THE EAST SEPARATED FROM ROME

At the end of the first millennium the final split occurred between the western church (which was now fully Roman Catholic) and the Eastern Orthodox churches. For several of the prior centuries, and despite the growing claims of the popes, there had been at least mutual respect. The popes had even thought it necessary to seek from the eastern emperor confirmation of their election to the pontificate. But a cleavage gradually developed, which came to a bitter climax in 1054, when a Roman delegation laid a bull of excommunication upon the altar of St Sophia in Constantinople. The Greek patriarch retaliated in kind, and the schism became complete. It was a sorry and absurd farce.

Two of the reasons for the rupture between the west and the east were -

QUARRELS OVER ICONS

Icons had become established in the east, but were little used in the west. The icons, with their suggestion of idolatry, had contributed to the ease of the Muslim conquests, and the conversion of thousands to Islam. Under pressure from the Muslims, and from the western churches, the Orthodox finally agreed not to use statues, and to confine icons to flat images of Christ, the virgin Mary, or of a saint. Those images were (and are) usually painted on boards, or carved in low relief.

Full veneration is given to icons in the Orthodox churches. Genuflections are made before them, incense is burned, invocations are directed to them. Orthodox Christians believe that icons are channels through which divine blessing flows to the faithful - pardon, healing, gracious answers to prayer. Miracles are believed to happen in the presence of icons, which for the faithful confirm their use.

The quarrel over icons was never fully resolved; except that now the situation exists where in Orthodox churches paintings are still the normal form of icon, while in Catholic and other churches both paintings and statues abound! Then, of course, thousands of Protestant churches contain neither.

THE "FILIOQUE" CONTROVERSY

This shameful quarrel (which still continues) became the actual flash-point that caused the final east-west schism. The west (headed by the pope) maintained that the Holy Spirit proceeded from both the Father and the Son (filioque = "and the Son"). But the east (headed by the patriarch) argued that he proceeded from the Father only (cp. John 15:26).

After several centuries of debate, the western doctrine was officially sanctioned by Pope Benedict VIII (in 1017), and the schism followed in 1054. All attempts to solve the problem since then have failed.

The western view (which is generally adopted by Protestants) is expressed in the western version of the Nicene Creed -

> "We believe in the Holy Spirit, who proceeds from both the Father and the Son"

The filioque clause was added to the creed near the end of the 6th century, against bitter opposition from the eastern churches. The western churches argued that the filioque

- ➢ preserves the union between the Father and the Son;
- ➢ preserves the union between the Son and the Spirit;
- ➢ accords with scripture.

The issue hardly seems to warrant the division it has caused; nonetheless, neither popes nor patriarchs were willing to yield ground to each other. Nor were they content to stand as equals, but insisted upon the right to final authority:

- ➢ the popes: because they claimed to occupy Peter's chair;
- ➢ the patriarchs: because Constantinople was the seat of the imperial court.

OTHER DIFFERENCES

The shifting boundaries caused by the collapse of the western Roman administration, the constant barbarian and Muslim invasions, the conflicting and changing alliances wrought by the popes and the emperors, brought Rome and Constantinople into frequent administrative and political conflict. This had the effect of exacerbating other differences between the two sees. Further, growing cultural and social differences, diverging languages, all made communications more difficult and more liable to misunderstanding. Then also a growing difference in the temperaments of the changing populations of eastern and western Europe enhanced the forces of separation. That difference is exemplified in their respective monastic developments: monasteries in the east tended to be more mystical, ascetic, contemplative; while those in the west were more pragmatic, activist, involved. But perhaps most of all, increasing liturgical differences between the churches of the west and the east made final separation more and more inevitable.

The papacy added its own pressure to the fissure by objecting with increasing vigour to the eastern emperor taking, or trying to take, authority over the church, or interfering in ecclesiastical affairs. By the end of the 8th century the popes no longer sought the emperor's confirmation of their enthronement; but the patriarchs, living within the boundaries of the empire, had little choice but to be subservient to the emperor. By contrast, as the papacy grew stronger, the popes demanded not only freedom from imperial interference, but also asserted their moral and religious authority over all civil and religious leaders, including ultimately the patriarch and the emperor.

JUSTINIAN I, THE GREAT

The Charismata

During this second half-millennium there are recurring references to the charismata; however, it also marked the end of the Montanists. Their demise was brought about by the Emperor Justinian I, a brilliant and able leader who in the 6th century restored both the eastern and western empires almost to their original glory under a single sceptre.

Justinian reigned for 38 years. He was married to Theodora, a former actress and courtesan, who nonetheless remained quite faithful to her husband and exerted a strong influence over him. Amazingly, we still have a portrait of her, set into a mosaic floor in a church in Ravenna. She was an exceptional woman. During a wild riot in Constantinople, when Justinian wanted to flee, she restrained him, and then alone confronted and tamed the mob. By that one act she saved his crown. She was so necessary to him, that when she died he lost interest in his empire, and much that he had achieved began to dissipate.

Justinian was an enthusiastic builder, but his greatest monument was the magnificent church of St Sophia, which still stands. For one thousand years it was a centre for Christian worship; then for five hundred years a Muslim mosque; and now for the past sixty years a museum of Byzantine art and culture.

During the time of his ascendancy, Justinian wanted to secure his restored dominions by uniting them in a single expression of the Christian faith, so by edicts, persuasion, and violence, he strove to compel all dissident groups to reenter the Catholic church. The Montanists, after four centuries, were still strong in Phrygia; but Justinian fell upon them with special vigour, and when they refused to yield, they were virtually exterminated.

What about glossolalia? The histories show that there was a widespread, although decreasing, occurrence of glossolalia well into the 4th century. After that date there are six centuries of silence; that is, there are no recorded instances of glossolalia from about the year 400 to the year 1000. There are, however, many references to other miracles, such as healings, exorcisms, visions, etc.

That silence does not mean that glossolalia vanished, for it probably continued in the lives of various saints and ascetics; but it certainly ceased to be common, and was officially frowned upon.

Glossolalia, and other charismata, appeared again in the Middle Ages (c. 1000-1600), and since then have never entirely vanished from the experience of the church.[156]

---

156 See the Addendum to this chapter.

The Virgin Mary

Apart from the nativity stories in Luke and Matthew, Mary occupies an insignificant role in the NT. There is nothing to indicate that the apostles gave her any special honour. How then has she come to occupy the exalted position she now has in Orthodox, and especially in Roman Catholic, doctrine? By them she is revered as the Mother of God, as co-mediatrix with Christ between God and man, and to many Catholics she is more personally real than the Saviour. Those are doctrines that bring a shudder to every Protestant soul.

In the face of vigorous Protestant protest, the Immaculate Conception of the Virgin was proclaimed by Rome in the mid-19th century, and her Assumption into heaven was made dogma by Pius XII in the mid-20th century. However, neither doctrine was invented at that time, but both had their roots in the distant past. In particular, the idea that Mary was perpetually a virgin has long been accepted as fact by millions of Christians.

For example the following astonishing account comes from an apocryphal gospel, composed in the late second century, barely a hundred years after the time of the apostles. The story-teller is supposedly Joseph, Mary's husband. He had found a midwife to help Mary in the delivery of her baby; but when the lady arrived she was overwhelmed by a luminous glow that filled the cave where the young mother was lying. After the blazing light had dimmed a little the midwife and Joseph realised that the baby was already born and was suckling at the breast. Now let Joseph take up the tale -

> "And the midwife cried out, and said: `This is a great day to me, because I have seen this strange sight.' And the midwife went forth out of the cave, and Salome met her. And she said to her: `Salome, Salome, I have a strange sight to relate to thee: a virgin has brought forth - a thing which nature admits not of.' Then said Salome: `As the Lord my

God liveth, unless I thrust in my finger, and search the parts, I will not believe that a virgin has brought forth.

"And the midwife went in and said to Mary: 'Show thyself, for no small controversy has arisen about thee.' And Salome put in her finger, and cried out, and said: 'Woe is me for mine iniquity

'and mine unbelief, because I have tempted the living God; and, behold, my hand is dropping off as if burned with fire!'"[157]

The story continues with Salome's lament, which came to an end only when an angel appeared and told her that God had forgiven her. But the thing to note here is the perhaps indelicate manner in which the story stresses that even after the birth of the baby, Mary was still a virgin.[158] Since there is no suggestion of such an idea in scripture, how did the tradition arise, and that so early?

---

157 The Protevangelium of James; "Ante-Nicene Fathers" Vol. 8; pg. 365,366. See the Index of the same volume, under "Mary", for a list of other extraordinary tales that developed very early around the life of the Virgin, from her infancy onward. For example:

-Mary's father was a very rich man, named Joachim; her mother was Anna; and she was born to them supernaturally after an angel visited them.

-six months after Mary was born she was able to walk unaided.

-at three years of age she was taken to the Temple where she lived until her betrothal to Joseph, and during this time she was miraculously fed by an angel.

158 That is, her hymen remained unbroken. A corollary assumption is that Mary never had sexual intercourse with Joseph, which is a strange proposition - see Mt 1:25. The gospel clearly implies that she and Joseph began normal marital relations after Jesus was born; and cp also Mt 12:46-50; Mk 6:3; etc.

THE SOURCES OF THE DOCTRINE

Various apocryphal gospels, that were at times more popular than the canonical gospels, gave Mary a much more exalted position than does scripture. These "gospels" were probably written to fill a supposed spiritual vacuum in the biblical accounts that troubled many pagans. To the average Greek and Roman convert, heaven seemed half-empty without a female deity; the supernatural stories about Mary nicely solved that problem.[159]

Another unfortunate development grew during the first centuries: Christ became increasingly remote from the people, hidden behind the panoply and power of the church. That remoteness was enhanced by another immensely popular set of apocryphal writings, known as the "infancy gospels". They ascribed all kinds of marvels to the boy Jesus, but thereby made him other than human. He became merely a deity in human disguise, like a Christian version of the pagan myths, but not really a sharer in our life.[160]

---

159 Note however, that the Bible does in fact ascribe feminine qualities to God, likening him to a mother as well as to a father. To cite just one example, see Mt 23:37.

160 See the Gospel of Pseudo-Matthew; the Gospel of Thomas; the Arabic Gospel; etc; "Ante-Nicene Fathers" Vol 8. 376/18,20; 380/33,34,38; 396/9-13; 398/2-5; 400/1; 413/42. See also the "Index" volume (Vol 9), column c. Some of the stories are

-the infant Christ miraculously purified muddy water; fashioned twelve sparrows from a soft clay and then made them fly away; cursed his enemies and made them suffer many things, but blessed and healed his friends.

-while he was not yet six years of age, Jesus raised another child from death, miraculously gathered up water spilled from a broken pitcher, and performed many other such prodigies.

-water in which the infant Christ was washed brought healing to a leprous girl; the ox and the ass in the stable bowed before him and worshipped him; when his parents took him to Egypt, and they were threatened by dragons, lions, and leopards, the baby walked and talked and compelled

Continued on next page...

By contrast with the increasingly ethereal Jesus, Mary seemed more accessible, more sympathetic. This attitude was enhanced by artists, who commonly portrayed Jesus as ethereal, ascetic, haloed, and quite apart from ordinary people.

As a way to exalt Christ, and to display his deity, the custom had developed by the 3rd century of calling Mary the "Theotokos" (Greek: "God-bearer"). Unhappily this was inaccurately translated into Latin as "Dei Genetrix" = "Mother of God". The effect was to reverse the emphasis of the original, placing it on Mary as the sacred mother, rather than upon the divinity of her child. That shifted emphasis became more and more fixed in the popular mind as the centuries passed.

The idea of Mary as "Mother of God" led almost inevitably to the idea of her perpetual virginity, which in turn led to the dogma of her own immaculate conception.

Another source of the exaltation of Mary was the custom of seeing her as a counterpart of Eve. Just as Eve was the active cause of our sinful state, so, it was argued, Mary must have an active part in our redemption. That argument developed into the idea of a

---

the wild animals to worship him; he commanded tall palm trees to bend down and yield their fruit to Mary; and so on, through many other bizarre and fantastic incidents.

-Jesus talked when he was still a baby (and cp. the Koran Sura 19:16-34); and to the above could be added:

-he terrified a band of robbers

-he supernaturally fed his mother

-he miraculously stretched some planks

-he made a dried fish live

-he turned children into goats

-he caused a snake to suck poison and burst

-he did many miracles of healing

-he humiliated some learned scribes

-he struck a boy dead, and then restored him; etc.

mediatorial role for Mary, especially when Christ was placed ever more distant from the people. Christ became an object of terror, but Mary of nurturing and sympathetic love. Yet, following the hierarchical structure of ancient society, her ascendancy was secured by ascribing to her the title "Our Lady", which became ever more popular, and by degrees was elevated almost to an equality with "Our Lord".

THE STABILISING OF THE DOCTRINE

All those trends were rationalised by the church, and eventually turned into dogma. As a result, Catholics now argue that there are three levels of worship:

- that due to God alone;
- that due to Mary; and
- that due to the saints.

They claim that they do not worship Mary as they worship Christ; but Protestants, observing the statuary, the shrines, the Rosary, the adoration that characterise popular attitudes to Mary, say that the Catholic argument about levels of worship is a distinction without a difference.

SUMMARY OF THE 500 YEARS

GREAT ADVANCES

The story of the second 500 years is not all gloom; for the church made great advances, sweeping whole nations into its arms, and spreading its influence throughout the known world. True, many of those converts were nominal; yet they were still exposed to the gospel, and good results often followed.

During that troubled period, Christianity showed remarkable resilience. Note that few (if any) religions (save perhaps Judaism) have been able to survive the destruction of their historical, natural, and cultural settings. Yet the church, in both east and west, emerged largely unscathed from the collapse of the Roman Empire, and went on to absorb the very people who had brought about that collapse. Even in Muslim lands the church, though much weakened, survived (and still does).

But during the second half-millennium there were also

GREAT LOSSES

In terms of its prominence in the total world scene, Christianity was actually less significant at the end of the 10th century than it had been 500 years earlier. Then, it had been the faith of virtually every citizen of the mightiest empire the Mediterranean world had seen, and also had many thousands of followers beyond the borders of that empire. But by the year 1000 many parts of that empire had been invaded and settled by barbarians who had not all become Christians, even in name. Islam also had conquered half of Rome's former territories, and now, only three centuries later, had added greatly to those territories and could boast more followers than could the church. Islam was also the dominant faith of several states more powerful than any of those in Europe at the turn of the millennium. Buddhism also, in contrast with a Christianity apparently then in decline, had enjoyed steady growth, and by the year 1000 was the dominant faith (along with Hinduism) of the many millions in Asia.

So an unbiased observer might well have thought that either Buddhism or Islam (more likely the latter) was destined to become the prevailing religion of mankind. That opinion would have been strengthened by the barbaric condition into which the states of Europe had fallen. Islamic, and especially Chinese cultures, were both at that time more advanced than those of any of the Christian states (including the eastern empire).[161]

---

161 As a cameo of the sophistication, beauty, and high culture of the Islamic world around the year 1000, let me quote just three quatrains (1, 12, 98) Continued on next page...

Yet that observer would have missed the real strength of the church, which is not found in its outward organisation, but in that spiritual company who comprise the true "body of Christ" on earth. While the visible church may have been in a state of constant fluctuation, that real church was experiencing steady growth throughout the entire period, and has never ceased from that growth. The continued and indestructible existence of that real church is the only guarantee of the ongoing success of the larger body.

RESURGENCE AND DECLINE

The next 500 years (1000-1500) saw a new explosion of energy in the church (especially in the west) that made Christianity the dominant faith in a larger part of the earth than any other religion had ruled prior to that time. That surge of life and growth was followed by another decline, which then led to the vast upheaval and reform caused by the Protestant Reformers, and on into the modern era of the church.

---

from the poetry of Omar Khayyam (c. 1050-c. 1123). Born a tent-maker's son, he became an astronomer, philosopher, poet, and renowned mathematician, whose works remained standard texts for many decades. Although Edward Fitzgerald's translation, quoted here, is generally said to be finer than the original Arabian version, it nonetheless reflects the essence of Muslim culture at that time -

Wake! For the Sun behind yon Eastern height
Has chased the Sessions of the Stars from Night;
And, to the field of Heav'n ascending, strikes

The Sultan's Turret with a Shaft of Light.
Here with a little Bread beneath the Bough,
A flask of Wine, a Book of Verse - and Thou
Beside me singing in the Wilderness -
Oh, Wilderness were Paradise enow!

Ah, with the Grape my fading Life provide,
And wash my Body whence the Life has died,
And lay me, shrouded in the Living Leaf,
By some not unfrequented Garden-side.

EPILOGUE

Let me close this major part of my book with a dramatic story. Just on one thousand years ago there was a long and bitter war between Christians and Muslims for possession of the island of Sicily - a war that the Christians won after a heroic struggle against superior forces. Here is an account of one of the battles, which occurred in 1063. The leader of the Christian forces was a young warrior, Count Roger of Calabria, who with only 60 knights and a small band of foot soldiers sailed across the strait between southern Italy and Sicily, and launched his invasion. The island had by that time been firmly in Saracen hands for nearly 200 years, with its capital at Palermo. The war was chronicled by Geoffrey of Malaterra, a Norman monk, who says that after some initial success against the Muslims

> "it was made known that the Berbers and the Arabs, together with the Sicilians, had arrived with a large army to wage war on Count Roger. ... For three days (the two armies) stared at one another with the river in between, neither side wanting to be the first to cross the river. On the fourth day, however, our forces, unwilling to allow the enemy to stay so close with impunity, made their confession before God with the utmost devotion in the presence of the priests and, having received absolution, advanced to attack the enemy, entrusting themselves to God's mercy and confident of his aid."

However, before the action was joined, word reached the Christians of another Muslim attack some distance away. The count sent off his nephew Serlo with just 36 men, to establish contact with the new foe, and to wait for a larger body of troops to arrive. But Serlo

> "not waiting for his uncle to arrive within the walls, burst upon the enemy like a raging lion and inflicted great slaughter among them, although they num-

> bered three thousand, not to mention the infantry, of whom there were an infinite number. A truly extraordinary event, for he with just 36 knights put them all to flight. This event enables us to recognise that God was our protector."

While this astonishing conflict was raging, the count arrived with his army, only to discover that many of his men were appalled when they saw the size of the enemy host, and they wanted to escape while they could. But he admonished them, and encouraged them, saying -

> "Keep up your spirits, you brave soldiers in Christ's army. We all bear the emblem of Christ, who will not desert his emblem, unless he is wronged. Our God, the God of gods, is all-powerful. Nor is it right to have doubts, for it is certain that, with God going before us, resistance is impossible."

So they took heart and launched their attack. As they advanced, they were wonderfully encouraged to see a knight, splendidly arrayed, and riding a magnificent white charger, appear in the vanguard of the small army to lead them into the battle. Seeing in this apparition a sign of heaven's favour, they marched on with enthusiasm and gained an absolute victory, for which they heartily praised God.[162]

I am far from advocating that we take up arms and enforce allegiance to Christ at the point of a sword, but rather want to echo the young count's sentiment that nothing is impossible for men and women who trust God. Whether our numbers are few or many, we are destined to triumph in Christ. He is building his church, against which not even the gates of hell can prevail. Let Satan war against us in whatever guise he pleases, he cannot prevail. The

---

162 Elizabeth Hallam, op. cit. pg. 49-51.

crown of glory is reserved for the all-conquering people of God, which people we are, by his grace toward us in Christ.

Addendum:
CHARISMATA ACROSS THE AGES

A.D. 41 AT CAESAREA

"While Peter yet spake these words, the Holy Ghost fell on all them which heard the word ... For they heard them speak with tongues, and magnify God." (Acts 10:44-46)

A.D. 54 AT EPHESUS

"And it came to pass, that, while Apollos was at Corinth, Paul having passed through the upper coasts came to Ephesus: and finding certain disciples, he said unto them: have ye received the Holy Ghost since ye believed? And they said unto him: We have not so much as heard whether there be any Holy Ghost. ... And when Paul had laid his hands upon them the Holy Ghost came upon them: and they spake with other tongues, and prophesied." (Acts 19:1-6)

A.D. 55 AT CORINTH

"Even so, ye, forasmuch as ye are zealous of spiritual gifts, seek that ye may excel to the edifying of the church. ... Therefore let him that speaketh in an unknown tongue pray that he may interpret. ... I thank my God that I (Paul) speak with tongues more than ye all." (1 Corinthians 14:12-18)

A.D. 100 EUSEBIUS (CHURCH HISTORIAN)

Writing to the preaching evangelists who were still living, Eusebius says: "Of those that flourished in these times, Quadratus is said to have been distinguished for his prophetical gifts. There were many others, who were also noted in these times who held rank in the Apostolic succession. ... The Holy Spirit also wrought many wonders as yet through them, so that as the Gospel was heard men in crowds voluntarily and eagerly embraced the true faith with their whole minds" ("Ecclesiastical History".)

A.D. 150 JUSTIN MARTYR (GREEK EVANGELIST)

(After the canon of scripture had closed.)

Reliable historians tell us that after the Scriptures were written the gift of speaking unknown languages continued on. About 100 years after the founding of the church, at a time when the Apostles were all dead and the Church dispensation was well under way, Justin Martyr wrote an apology to Trypho the Jew: "If you want proof that the Spirit of God, who was with your people and left you to come to us, come into our assemblies and there you will see him cast out demons, heal the sick and hear him speak in tongues" (Morris Plotts - "Herald of Faith".)

A.D. 115 TO 202 IRENAEUS

He was a pupil of Polycarp, who was a disciple of the Apostle John. He wrote in his book "Against Heresies" (Book V,VI): "In like manner we do also hear many brethren in the church who possess prophetic gifts, and who, through the Spirit, speak all kinds of languages, and bring to light for the general benefit the hidden things of men and declare the mysteries of God, whom also the apostles term spiritual."

ROBERT NORTON

Robert Norton was able to quote the following significant testimony of Irenaeus: "The true disciples of Jesus Christ (says he) receiving favours from Him, perform works for the benefit of other men, as every one hath received the gift from Him. For some cast out devils. Others have the knowledge of things future, and visions, and prophecies. Others by the laying on of their hands, heal the sick, and restore their health. Also, as we have said before, even the dead are raised, and have continued with us many years." (Robert Norton - "Historic Review of Miraculous Manifestations in the Church of Christ" - London, 1839, pp 342, 343)

A.D. 200 TERTULLIAN OF CARTHAGE

Tertullian (one of the most eminent men the church has produced) speaks about the spiritual gifts, including the gift of tongues, and says they were manifest among the Montanists, to which he belonged ("Signs Following", page 328.)

Montanus, who began prophesying in A.D. 172, developed an apocalyptic movement which lived in expectation of the speedy outpouring of the Holy Spirit on the church. The movement was, in many ways, a reaction to the then growing institutionalism and secularism of the church. The Latin Father, Tertullian, was prepared to give his allegiance to the movement ("Bakers' Dict. Theol." 1966, p. 363.)

Referring to the Montanist, John Wesley in his journal of 15th August, 1750, writes: "By reflecting on an old book which I had read in the journey, I was fully convinced of what I had long suspected: that the Montanists in the second and third centuries were real scriptural Christians; and that the grand reason why the miraculous gifts were so soon withdrawn was, not only that faith and holiness were well nigh lost, but that dry, formal, orthodox men began even then to ridicule whatever gifts they had not themselves, and to decry them all, as either madness or imposture."

Tertullian also taught that there was a considerable difference between the church consisting of a number of Bishops and the church of the Spirit which manifests itself through men enlightened by the Holy Spirit ("History of the Christian Religion", 1851, Volume 11, page 211.)

A.D. 258 CYPRIAN

The Bishop of Carthage, martyred A.D. 258, wrote: "The discipline of God over us never ceases, both by night and day, to correct and reprove; for not only by the visions of the night, but by day, even the innocent age of children is filled among us with the Holy Spirit; and they see, and hear and speak in ecstasy such things as the Lord vouchsafes to admonish and instruct us by" ("History of the Christian Religion", 1851, Volume 11, page 345.)

Eusebius of Caesarea, the famous church historian, who lived about A.D. 260-340, in his "Church History", Book III, p. 37, writes: "The Holy Spirit wrought many wonders through them, so that vast crowds, at the first hearing of the Gospel, eagerly received it into their hearts."

A.D. 300 THE EARLY MARTYRS

The early martyrs enjoyed these gifts. Dean Farrar in his book, "Darkness to Dawn" states: "Even for the minutest allusions and particulars I have contemporary authority." He refers to the persecuted Christians in Rome singing and speaking in unknown tongues.

A.D. 300 CHRYSOSTOM OF CONSTANTINOPLE

Chrysostom, Bishop of Constantinople writes: "Whoever was baptised in Apostolic days, he straightaway spoke with tongues, for since on their coming over from idols, without any clear knowledge or training in the Scriptures, they at once received the Spirit; not that they saw the Spirit, for he is invisible, but God's grace bestowed some sensible proof of His energy, and one straightaway spoke in the Persian language, another in the Roman, another in the Indian, another in some other tongue, this made to them that were without (that is, outside the company of the disciples) that it was the Spirit in every person (who was) speaking (through them in other tongues). Wherefore the Apostle calls it the manifestation of the Spirit which is given to every man to profit withal." ("With Signs Following", S. H. Frodsham, p. 327.)

A.D. 330-379 BASIL THE GREAT

In his writing on the Spirit he says: "The gifts of the Spirit, including the diversities of tongues, are in the church. The church being the appointed depository of the gifts that are of the Holy Spirit" ("The Nicene and Post-Nicene Fathers", 2nd Series, op. cit. Volume 9, page 147.)

A.D. 400 AUGUSTINE OF HIPPO[163]

Augustine, Bishop of Hippo, one of the four great fathers of the Latin church, and considered the greatest of them all, says: "We still do what the Apostles did when they laid hands on the Samaritans and called down the Holy Spirit on them in the laying on of hands. It is expected that converts should speak with new tongues."

THE DARK AGES

Even in the dark ages, God gave some gracious revivals. From the 12th to the 15th Century there were revivals in Southern Europe in which many spoke in other tongues. Foremost among these revivalists were the Waldenses and the Albigenses.

---

163 See again the first footnote to this Addendum.

PART THREE:

THE UNIVERSAL CHURCH (A.D. 1000-2000)

by EARL E. CAIRNE (Ph.D)

HISTORY IS BUNK?

The great motor magnate Henry Ford is renowned for many things, including being called the author of the epigram, "History is bunk!" He has been unfairly condemned. What he actually said, in an interview published in the Chicago Tribune (May 25, 1916), was this:

> "History is more or less bunk. It's tradition. We don't want tradition. We want to live in the present, and the only history that is worth a tinker's damn is the history we make today."

Who would not rather be a maker of history than merely a reader of it? Certainly, to shape the contours of time is the task God has laid on his church; not to turn to the world (as the Lord growled at Jeremiah), but to force the world to turn to the church (Je 15:19); to move mountains, not be crushed by them (Mk 11:22-24).

Nonetheless (if I may quote Santayana's aphorism a second time), "Those who cannot remember the past are condemned to repeat it."[164] There is no sensible way to understand the present or advance into the future without some awareness of the past. So although the major part of my book is now written (the first one thousand years), it is needful to round out the story with at least an outline of the next one thousand years and bring it up to our own time. Hence the next two chapters.

Please note that I am not the author of the remainder of this book. These two final chapters have been taken from a set of lecture notes prepared by an American teacher, Dr Earl E. Cairne. Although they are skeletal they will give you a clear but concise view of the second millennium of Christian witness worldwide.

---

[164] See the second paragraph of Chapter Three above. In one of my sources the word "repeat" is replaced by "fulfil".

Chapter Eleven:
MEDIAEVAL CHURCH

RELIGIOUS ZEAL IN THE WEST[165]

RISE OF THE ORTHODOX CHURCH

John of Damascus (eighth century) systematised conciliar theology (325-451) in his Fountain of Knowledge.

Separation of the eastern and western Churches resulted from disputes over the date of Easter, conflict after 726 over images in the church, which the Orthodox Church rejected, and over the use of unleavened bread in the Mass

> - this last dispute was one occasion for the Schism of 1054 which created the Orthodox Church.

The Orthodox Church won the Russians under Vladimir in 989 and the Moravians through the missionary work of Methodius and Cyril.

THE GROWING STRENGTH OF THE PAPACY

The eighth century Donation of Constantine supported papal control of land in Italy and the mid-ninth century Pseudo-Isidorian Decretals buttressed the power of the pope over churchmen.

Ansgar's work helped eventually to bring Scandinavia under papal control.

---

[165] Note once again that this chapter and the next are the work of Dr Earle E. Cairne (Ph.D). They are outline notes prepared for VCC in the USA, and are included here just to round out the story of the church and bring it up to our time.

Radbertus' teaching of the idea of transubstantiation made the Mass the major means of grace.

The centralised Cluniac Congregation of Monds after 931 supported reform and religious independence from lay control.

Able popes, such as Nicholas I, upheld and enforced standards of morality upon powerful rulers and church leaders.

PAPAL VICTORIES (1054-1305)

THE PEAK OF PAPAL POWER

The Lateran Council of 1059 permitted the College of Cardinals to elect the pope.

Gregory VII (Hildebrand), in keeping with the spirit of Dictatus Papae, which upheld papal supremacy, put down simony, clerical marriage, and humiliated Henry IV, the Holy Roman emperor, at Canossa in 1076 in a dispute over investiture

➤ this was finally ended in a compromise at Worms in 1122.

Innocent III (1198-1216) humbled Philip Augustus of France in a dispute over divorce and John of England in a clash over the appointment of the Archbishop of Canterbury and brought the Holy Roman emperor under his control

he sponsored the Fourth Crusade, which captured Constantinople and set up a Latin kingdom (1204-1261) and a crusade against the Albigensians

he had the Fourth Lateran Council (1215) assert transubstantiation and annual confession.

CRUSADES AND REFORMS

➤ Crusades were directed against the Moors in Spain, the Albigenses of France and the Moslems in Palestine

- Crusaders mainly went to Palestine for religious reasons, to accomplish the Christian reconquest of Palestine, and to aid the Eastern Empire against Moslem pressure.
- the First Crusade had two parts, the lay crusade, which was a failure; and the crusade of feudal lords, who set up the Latin kingdom of Jerusalem (1099-1187)
- the Fourth Crusade created the Latin kingdom of Constantinople (1204-1261) thus deepening the animosity between the eastern and western Churches.
- the Crusades failed to hold Palestine permanently, strengthened the power of national rulers, weakened the eastern Empire, and acquainted the West with Greco-Moslem learning and culture.

Monastic reform came through the monks of the new Cistercian order, led by the godly Bernard of Clairvaux, mystic, hymn-writer (e.g. "Jesus the Very Thought of Thee") and theologian

- also through the military orders (Knights of Templars and Knights Hospitallers)
- also through the mendicants or friars of the missionary-minded Franciscan order (of Francis of Assisi)
- and through the educator-mendicants of the Dominican Order, such as Thomas Aquinas and Savonarola.

Lay movements arose; some with a philosophical basis, such as the Cathari or Albigensians (whose ideas resembled those of the Gnostics); and some with a Biblical basis, such as the Waldensian Movement of Peter Waldo in Italy

- the Church used crusades, a ban on the use of the Bible, and the Inquisition, against the latter two.

MEDIAEVAL CULTURE

SCHOLASTICISM

This was an attempt to reconcile the natural philosophy of Aristotle and Biblical revelation; it used Aristotle's logic and philosophy to synthesise the canon, creeds and writ of the church Fathers.

The realists, such as Anselm, who wrote Cur Deus Homo on the atonement, and the Monologium, a deductive argument for the existence of God, believed that Ideas existed before created things

- that is, faith precedes reason.

Moderate realists, such as Aquinas in his Summa Theologiae, believed that one used reason to the point where faith must take over to reach such ideas as the Incarnation and Trinity

- Aquinas' theology is the official position of the Roman Catholic church.

The nominalists such as William of Occam, denied the objective existence of ideas, except as class names for things, and separated faith and reason.

Realists and moderate realists put the corporate organisation and hierarchy of the Church above the individual. Nominalism, leaving theological authority to the Church so emphasised human learning and activity by the individual that it stimulate science and mysticism.

UNIVERSITIES AROSE IN THIS ERA

- around great teachers, such as Abelard in Paris
- as cathedral schools, such as that of Notre Dame
- from student migrations, such as that from Paris to Oxford.

Attempts To Reform The Church
INTERNAL REFORMERS

Many things led to a demand for reform:
- the immorality of many clergymen
- feudalism, which secularised the Church by creating a dual allegiance
- heavy papal taxes and fees
- the rise of nation-states whose rulers were opposed to the interference of a universal Church in national affairs
- the Babylonian Captivity during which popes resided at Avignon instead of Rome from 1309 to 1377
- and the Great Schism between 1378 and 1417 (when there were rival popes at Avignon and Rome).

Internal reform was attempted by:
- mystics who sought direct communion with God
- one of the Friends of God wrote the Theologia Germanica which helped Martin Luther
- from the Brethren of the Common Life came the Imitation of Christ.
- John Wycliffe of England changed from reform of the clergy to attacks on papal authority and the mass after 1387
- he began an English translation of the Bible, founded the Lollards and influenced Huss of Bohemia, whose ideas resulted in the founding of the United Brethren.

Between 1409 and 1449 reforming councils, representative of the Church as suggested by Marsillus in Defensor Pacis, sought at Pisa to end the Great Schism, put down heresy, and reform the Church

- ➤ the Council at Constance selected a new pope to replace the three claimants, burned Huss and asserted its authority above the pope
- ➤ the papacy finally defeated this attempt to give the Church a constitutional instead of an absolute monarchy.

The Renaissance in <u>Teutonic</u> lands stressed biblical sources. But in <u>Italy</u> Leo X under classical influence rebuilt St Peter's in Rome, and Nicholas V began the Vatican library

- ➤ Reuchlin's Hebrew Grammar and Dictionary and Erasmus' Greek New Testament (1516) enabled scholars to compare the mediaeval and early churches to the disadvantage of the former
- ➤ Erasmus critical works, such as In Praise of Folly, demanded reform.

Chapter Twelve:
MODERN CHURCH

MODERN CHURCH HISTORY (1517 TO 1900)
WIDESPREAD REFORMATION (1517-1648)
THE CAUSES

The reformation was a revolt in <u>polity</u> from the universal Church but a reformation in <u>doctrine</u> based on Biblical patterns

- ➤ the direct cause was Martin Luther's protest in his 95 Theses (October 31, 1517) against the abuse of indulgences as practised by Tetzel under the sponsorships of Albert and Leo X.

THE LUTHERAN REFORMATION

The Nominalist teaching of William of Occam, who denied to reason any real role in theology, the spiritual guidance of Staupitz, a visit to Rome, the Theologia Germanica, and studies of his Bible as professor at the University of Wittenberg were indirect influences in Luther's conversion and break with Rome

- ➤ after conferences failed to heal the breach, Luther attacked the Mass, the hierarchy and theology of Rome in his three pamphlets of 1520

- ➤ this brought about his excommunication, and, in 1521 at the Diet of the Holy Roman Empire at Worms, the declaration that he was an outlaw

- ➤ while in hiding in Wartburg he translated the New Testament into German.

The creed of the emerging Lutheran Church, the Augsburg Confession of Melanchthon, appeared in 1530

- in 1535 Lutheran ordination to the ministry began.

War between Protestant and Roman Catholic princes was settled by the toleration of Lutheranism in the Peace of Augsburg, 1555.

Disputes in Lutheranism led to the definitive Formula of Concord and the Book of Concord.

Luther's theology, his hymns (such as "A Mighty Fortress"), his stress on education to read the Bible in the vernacular, were carried to Denmark by Hans Tausen; and to Norway, Iceland, Finland, and to Sweden by Olavus Petri, with the help of the ruler, who liberated Sweden from Denmark.

THE REFORMED FAITH

Reformation in Switzerland, with its democratic and humanistic tradition, came to Zurich and Berne in the North through Zwingli's debates with Roman Catholics and formal decrees by the city councils

- Farel and Calvin in the south brought Reformed ideas to Geneva after Calvin published his Institutes of the Christian Religion (1536), which emphasised the sovereignty of God
- his Ecclesiastical Ordinances (1541) created a church which influenced state action and administered moral discipline on all citizens.

The Huguenots, who created a Reformed church in France in 1559, were the target of the horrible Massacre of St Bartholomew's Day and became embroiled in a series of religious wars

- the Edict of Nantes in 1598 gave them toleration until 1685, when its revocation forced them to emigrate.

John Knox between 1560 and 1567, with the aid of Scottish nobles and middle class merchants, defeated Mary Stuart's attempt to keep

Scotland in the Roman fold and created a church which was Calvinistic in theology and Presbyterian in polity.

The fight to establish the Reformed faith in Holland was linked with the bloody fight to gain independence from Spain

- ➢ the former was achieved by 1571 and the latter by 1581
- ➢ William of Orange was the great patriot leader
- ➢ Jacobus Arminius, who opposed Calvinism as making God the Author of sin and man an automaton, believed that election was based on foreknowledge, the atonement was unlimited and grace resistible
- ➢ the Synod of Dort decided against the Arminian position but Arminianism lives on in Methodism and other groups.

Reformed theology was brought to Northern Ireland by James 1 who planted Scottish Presbyterians in Northern Ireland after 1603

- ➢ this partly explains the present division of Ireland.

Calvinism also spread to Hungary, Bohemia, and the German Palatinate.

THE ANABAPTISTS

Anabaptists emerged in Zurich in 1521 when Conrad Grebel and others opposed infant baptism into a state church and favoured adult baptism into a church of believers.

Persecution in Zurich spread the movement throughout the Holy Roman Empire, although the millennarian views, and communal polygamous acts of John of Leyden in Munster in 1535 gave it a bad name

- ➢ Menno Simons in Holland organised the refugees into a church, which held to the ideas of a pure church, adult believers' baptism, the Bible authority, and the separation of church and state.

ANGLICANISM, PURITANISM AND JANSENISM

Henry VIII created a national Catholic church by the Act of Supremacy because the pope would not grant him a divorce from Catherine to marry Anne Boleyn who, he hoped would give him a male heir.

- the English clergy under Thomas Cranmer gave him the divorce.

Henry supported Roman Catholic doctrine in the Six Articles but despoiled the monasteries and gave the people a vernacular Bible based on Tyndale's and Coverdale's work.

- a Protestant Church developed in Edward VI's reign; Crammer developed its creed (The 42 Articles) and the prayer book
- Mary sought to re-establish the Roman Catholic religion, but her marriage to Philip of Spain and martyrdom at the stake of nearly 300 people helped to make England Protestant
- Elizabeth created the Anglican system by the adoption of The 39 Articles and the Book of Common Prayer
- the Papal threat was ended by the defeat of the Spanish Armada in 1588.

Puritans opposed Elizabeth's settlement as too "Romish" and wanted Calvinistic theology, a Presbyterian (Thomas Cartwright), or Congregational (Henry Jacob) state church, simpler liturgy and clerical garments, and strict keeping of Sunday.

- separatists, following Robert Browne, wanted each church to be one of believers united to Christ and each other by a covenant
- John Robinson's Scrooby Congregation, which settled in Plymouth, held this opinion

- General Baptists, influenced by Mennonites in Holland, held to affusion and Arminianism; but the Particular Baptists who separated from Jacob's Church in 163 adopted Calvinism and immersion.

These Puritan forces cooperated against James I who approved the translation of the King James Version.

- nearly 20,000 went to New England between 1629 and 1640; the rest, under Oliver Cromwell, and as the result of a royal attempt to force the Book of Common Prayer on Scotland, engaged in civil war with Charles I and executed him in 1649
- the Westminster Assembly gave to Presbyterianism its confession, Cathechisms, form of government, Book of Worship
- the restoration of Charles II in 1660 ended the Puritan movement but not its influence.

THE COUNTER REFORMATION

The Oratory of Divine Love, a group of Roman Catholic leaders, sought to deepen spiritual life and bring reform.

Religious orders, such as the Thetines, which bound secular priests by the threefold monastic vow, served the people.

Popes, such as Paul III, approved the Jesuit order, the Inquisition, and the Index of Prohibited Books, while the rulers of the Holy Roman Empire and Spain, especially Philip II, supported the Church with armed force.

- the Inquisition, modelled upon the Spanish pattern, was used against heretics
- the Index was a list of books Roman Catholics could not read.

The Jesuit order founded by Ignatius Loyola, was absolutely obedient to the Pope and helped to reconquer Poland.

The Council of Trent (1545-63) adopted Thomistic theology as that of the Church and the Vulgate of Jerome as its authorised Bible.

THE THIRTY YEARS WAR

It was caused by the exclusion of Calvinists from toleration in the Empire, by Jesuit interference in politics, and by the rise of rival leagues of princes.

- a dispute in Prague was the occasion for war.
- the Bohemian and Danish phases were victories for Rome; the Swedish phase freed north Germany from Rome; and the final French phase led to peace.

The Treaty of Westphalia (1648) recognised Calvinism, and for the first time in modern history enshrined in law the idea of religious toleration.

THE RESULTS OF THE REFORMATION

- National Protestant churches replaced the universal church in countries
- Protestants accepted the authority of the Bible, justification by faith and the priesthood of believers
- numerous Protestant creeds were formulated.
- Three-level systems of education were set up.
- Political equality was taught by many Calvinists.
- Capitalism was stimulated.
- Preaching was revived.

DEISM, DENOMINATIONS AND REVIVALS (1648-1789)

COLONIAL AMERICAN CHRISTIANITY

Directors of the Virginia Company brought settlers with the Anglican ministers to Virginia. Blair and Bray improved the colonial ministry. Anglicanism also became the established church in New York, Maryland, South and North Carolina, and Georgia.

New England Congregationalism grew out of the migration of the Scrooby Separatists to Plymouth in 1620, and of the Massachusetts Bay Company stockholders to Salem and Boston to form Massachusetts Colony. Later Thomas Hooker and his friends from Massachusetts and Davenport's Bible commonwealth united to form Connecticut. The Cambridge Platform of 1648 decreed Calvinistic theology and congregational polity for these churches.

Rhode Island Baptists emerged from the enforced migrations Roger Williams and Anne Hutchinson for insistence on separation of church and state and freedom of conscience.

For economic reasons the Calverts founded Maryland as a colony with religious toleration.

Quakerism took roots in West Jersey and Pennsylvania where religious freedom drew many sects.

Swedish Lutherans in Delaware and later in Pennsylvania were united by Muhlenburg.

Francis Makemie established a Presbyterianism augmented by Scotch Settlers (Scotch-Irish) 1710-1750).

Robert Strawbridge and Philip Embury planted Methodism, which was organised by Francis Asbury.

Higher education was fostered to provide leaders in church and state by founding of Harvard (1636), William and Mary (1696), Yale (1701), Princeton (1746), Brown (1764, Rutgers (1825), and Haverford (1833).

THE GREAT AWAKENING

The Great Awakening began in the Middle Colonies with Frelinghuysen's and Gilbert Tennent's preaching, spread to New England by the efforts of Jonathan Edwards, Calvinism's defender, and to the South among Presbyterians, Methodists, and Baptists. Whitefield was the co-ordinator. Revival resulted in new members, colleges, and schisms.

Most churches, except the neutral Methodists and pacifist Quakers, supported the Revolution. Separation of church and state began in Virginia.

DEISM AND REVIVAL

Deism, the result of Newtonian science, Lockean psychology, and rationalistic philosophy, was a natural religion whose dogmas as stated by Herbert of Cherbuty were belief in a transcendent God, an Ethical life and immortality with rewards and punishment. It spread to North America and the Continent. Man's goodness and perfectibility were stressed.

Biblical revivalism was manifested in

The Pietist revival through the efforts of Philip Spencer in German Lutheranism. The Moravian Church under Zinzendorf and the revitalising of German Lutheranism were results.

Whitefield and the Wesleys revived lower-class England and after John Wesley's death the Arminian and socially-minded Methodist Church emerged.

Inner light revivalism appeared through George Fox, the founder of English Quakerism. Robert Barclay, its theologian, declared that the inner light provided men with continuing inspiration and revelation.

ROMANISM, MISSIONS AND LIBERALISM (1789-1914)

ROMAN CATHOLICISM suffered setbacks during the French Revolution; but aided by the Jesuit order, and the able Pious IX, who declared the Immaculate Conception of Mary in 1854 and the dogma of papal infallibility at the Vatican Council in 1870, it made great gains. After 1870, loss of the Papal States to a united Italy and anti-clerical legislation in Germany, France and other lands again weakened it.

The ANGLICAN CHURCH consisted of:

Upper class Evangelicals including ministers, such as Newton, the "Clapham Sect" of Wilberforce, and others interested in evangelism and social reforms. They espoused the abolition of the slave-trade (1807) and slavery (1833) and improvement of the social and economic condition of workers (Shaftesbury).

The Broad church with Biblical critics as Bishop Colenso or Christian socialists as Charles Kingsley.

The Oxford Movement of John Keble, Edward Pusey, and John Newman

> ➢ he and nearly 900 others became Roman Catholics - which emphasised ritualism and sacramentalism.

Booth's Salvation Army (1878), John Darby's Plymouth Brethren and George Williams' Y.M.C.A. were new nonconformist organisations.

English missionaries, beginning with William Carey in 1792, who were sent out and supported by newly organised societies, became missionary explorers (Livingston opened Africa and fought the slave trade), linguists (Moffat), and missionary statesmen (Tucker brought Uganda into the British Empire).

Patronage, the right of the Crown of landowners to appoint ministers, and revivalism led to schisms in Scottish Presbyterianism, such as the revivalistic Free Church of Thomas Chalmers.

In 1869 Roman Catholics were aided by the disestablishment of the Anglican Church in Ireland.

NEW FOES OF THE CHURCH

Idealistic philosophy making the Bible only an historic book to be analysed by Biblical critics, such as Wellhausen and Baur, resulted in a Bible which only contained God's Word.

Darwinian evolution denied original sin and stimulated the concept of the evolution of religion.

The atheistic and materialistic system of Communism set fort in the Communist Manifesto of Marx and Engels was to become a bitter foe to Christianity.

NATIONAL AMERICAN CHRISTIANITY

The Second Awakening, beginning at Yale under Timothy Dwight after 1789, spread on the frontier by the new camp meeting technique (Cane Ridge, 1801). It resulted in new churches such as the Disciples and the Unitarians, new seminaries, such as Andover, and foreign missions through Adoniram Judson's work.

Social reforms, such as temperance and the abolition of slavery, were supported by the church.

Schisms over slavery split Methodists, Presbyterians and Baptists.

Joseph Smith's Mormonism and William Miller's Adventism were new frontier sects, and Mrs Eddy's Christian Science as well as spiritualism emerged in the cities.

Rural and foreign immigration into industrial cities brought problems which the Church tried to solve by rescue missions, social settlements (Hull House), the Y.M.C.A., and the institutional church to meet the needs of the whole man. Walter Rauschenbusch's social gospel sought to improve conditions by democratic action in economic and political life.

Horace Bushnell's Christian Nurture (1847) stressed religious education as a substitute for evangelism of children, and John Vincent's uniform lessons stimulated the growth of Sunday Schools.

THE TWENTIETH CENTURY CHURCH

THE CHURCH AND STATE

The church in World War II, while engaging in humanitarian and religious activity, did not become the chauvinistic, bond-selling, recruiting, hate-Germany organisation it was in World War I.

Roman Catholicism, which suffered losses from Communism and desertion by Latin American intellectuals, sought to regain ground by accommodations with Mussolini and Hitler, by courting the U.S.A. and by the new dogma of Mary's Assumption (1950).

Communism in Russian and elsewhere fought Christianity by state legislation, atheistic propaganda and persecution.

ABSOLUTISM AND ECUMENICALISM

Imminental, relativistic, and subjective liberalism was opposed by a turn-around in theology evidenced in:

Conservatism negatively opposing evolution (Scopes Case) and liberalism (Machen) positively promoting apologetic literature (e.g. The Fundamentals, Bible schools (Moody) and colleges (Wheaton, Ill).

New-orthodoxy, begun by Karl Barth, accepted liberal Biblical criticism but advocated a transcendent God known by the Holy Spirit revealing Christ in the Bible. It stimulated a return of biblical theology.

Neo-Thomism attempted to accommodate the theology of Aquinas to modern science and the problems of our century.

New Cults, such as Unity, Jehovah's Witness, and the Oxford Group of Buhan, offer absolutist panaceas to modern problems.

Ecumenicalism began with:

- ➢ interdenominational co-operation in youth organisations, such as the International Missionary Council, or Evangelical Foreign Mission Association.

- ➢ it was stimulated by organic reunion of like denominations, such as the Methodist Church in 1939, and unlike denominations, such as the United Church of Canada.

- ➢ ecumenical confederation, begun with the doctrinally based Evangelical Alliance (1846) has resulted in loose confederations of like denominations, e.g. the Lutheran World Federation. Liberalism and New-orthodoxy have promoted local confederated churches, national confederations, such as the National Council (1950- organised as the Federal Council, 1908) and the International World Council of Churches, 1950). Evangelicals have countered with organisations such as the National Association of Evangelicals and the World Evangelical Fellowship.

BIBLIOGRAPHY

Chronicles of the Crusades; ed. Elizabeth Hallam; Weidenfeld and Nicolson, London, 1989.

Churches Aglow Down the Ages; Charles Taylor; Pub. by the author; 1991.

Documents of the Christian Church; ed. Henry Bettenson; Oxford University Press, London, 1975.

Early Christian Writings, tr. Maxwell Staniforth; Penguin Books, London, 1968.

Ecclesiastical History of the English People; by the Venerable Bede (673-675); tr. by Leo Sherley-Price; Penguin Classics, London, 1990.

Ecclesiastical History; Bohn's Ecclesiastical Library; London,

Encyclopaedia Americana, The; Latourette; 1959.

Foxe's Book of Martyrs; ed. Marie Gentert King; Fleming H. Revell Co, NJ, 1976.

Gibbon's Decline and Fall of the Roman Empire; abridged by Rosemary Wilson; Bison Books Ltd, London, 1991.

History of Christianity, A (in 5 vols); Vol 1, *The First Five Centuries;* Zondervan Pub. House.

History of Christianity, A; Kenneth S. Latourette; Harper & Row; 1975.

History of the Expansion of Christianity, A, vol 2, by K. S. Latourette.

Josephus: Complete Works, *Wars of the Jews;* tr. by William Whiston; 1977 reprint of the original 1867 work; Kregel Publications, Grand Rapids.

Koran, The

Life of Jesus; French essayist and historian (1823-1892); *Introduction* 1863..

New Eusebius, A; ed. J. *Stevenson*; S.P.C.K., London, 1975.

Nicene and Post-Nicene Fathers, *Second Series*, Vol 8; Eerdmans Publishing Co.; 1978 reprint.

Oracles Galore; Ken Chant; Vision Publishing.

Oxford Book of Prayer, The; ed. George *Appleton*; Oxford University Press, Oxford; 1985.

Oxford Dictionary of Saints, The; ed. David Hugh Farmer; Oxford University Press, Oxford, 1987.

Pillow Book of Sei Shonagon, The; tr. by Ivan Morris; Penguin Classics, 1967.

Quo Vadis?; *Whither Goest Thou?*; Henryk Sienkiewicz.

Religio Medici; *The Faith of a Physician*;Sir Thomas Browne; (1605-82) J. M. Dent & Sons Ltd.London; 1956.

The Georgics – *Introduction*; (Publius Vergilius Maro); tr. K. R. Mackenzie; The Folio Society, London, 1969.

Visions of the End; *Apocalyptic Traditions in the Middle Ages;* From a Homily on Ezekiel 2:6.; Bernard McGinn; Columbia University Press, New York, 1979.

Windsor Castle; W. H. Ainsworth; *Introduction;* by John Moore; Heron Books, London; undated.

Worship Leader, The; Ken Chant; Vision Publishing.

www.ingramcontent.com/pod-product-compliance
Lightning Source LLC
Chambersburg PA
CBHW071702090426
42738CB00009B/1631